IRAN IRAQ WAR

Gary E. McCuen

IDEAS IN CONFLICT SERIES

publications inc.

502 Second Street
Hudson, Wisconsin 54016

Illustration & photo credits
Carol Simpson 117, Iranian War Department 41, 49, 55, 67, 78, 93, 124, Iraqi Foreign Ministry 71, Sack 37, Sanders 85, Dana Summers 37, Ron Swanson 13, 18, 112, The WREE View of Women 25, 31, 98

© 1987 by Gary E. McCuen Publications, Inc.
502 Second Street • Hudson, Wisconsin 54016
(715) 386-7113
International Standard Book Number 0-86596-060-7
Printed in the United States of America

CONTENTS

CHAPTER 4   THE GULF WAR AND U.S. POLICY

REASONING SKILL DEVELOPMENT

These activities may be used as individualized study guides for students in libraries and resource centers or as discussion catalysts in small group and classroom discussions.

IDEAS in CONFLICT ®

This series features ideas in conflict on political, social and moral issues. It presents counterpoints, debates, opinions, commentary and analysis for use in libraries and classrooms. Each title in the series uses one or more of the following basic elements:

Introductions that present an issue overview giving historic background and/or a description of the controversy.

Counterpoints and debates carefully chosen from publications, books, and position papers on the political right and left to help librarians and teachers respond to requests that treatment of public issues be fair and balanced.

Symposiums and forums that go beyond debates that can polarize and oversimplify. These present commentary from across the political spectrum that reflect how complex issues attract many shades of opinion.

A global emphasis with foreign perspectives and surveys on various moral questions and political issues that will help readers to place subject matter in a less culture-bound and ethno-centric frame of reference. In an ever shrinking and interdependent world, understanding and cooperation are essential. Many issues are global in nature and can be effectively dealt with only by common efforts and international understanding.

Reasoning skill study guides and discussion activities provide ready made tools for helping with critical reading and evaluation of content. The guides and activities deal with one or more of the following:

RECOGNIZING AUTHOR'S POINT OF VIEW

INTERPRETING EDITORIAL CARTOONS

VALUES IN CONFLICT

WHAT IS EDITORIAL BIAS?

WHAT IS SEX BIAS?
WHAT IS POLITICAL BIAS?
WHAT IS ETHNOCENTRIC BIAS?
WHAT IS RACE BIAS?
WHAT IS RELIGIOUS BIAS?

*From across **the political spectrum** varied sources are presented for research projects and classroom discussions. Diverse opinions in the series come from magazines, newspapers, syndicated columnists, books, political speeches, foreign nations, and position papers by corporations and non-profit institutions.*

About the Editor
Gary E. McCuen is an editor and publisher of anthologies for public libraries and curriculum materials for schools. Over the past 16 years his publications of over 200 titles have specialized in social, moral and political conflict. They include books, pamphlets, cassettes, tabloids, filmstrips and simulation games, many of them designed from his curriculums during 11 years of teaching junior and senior high school social studies. At present he is the editor and publisher of the *Ideas in Conflict* series and the *Editorial Forum* series.

CHAPTER 1

THE PAST AND THE PRESENT

1   PAST AND PRESENT

IRAN AND IRAQ: HISTORICAL OVERVIEW

Bureau of Public Affairs

Iran

The ancient nation of Iran, historically known to the West as Persia, has been overrun frequently and has had its territory altered throughout the centuries. Invaded by Arabs, Seljuk Turks, Mongols, and others—and often caught up in the affairs of larger powers—Iran has always reasserted its national individuality and has emerged from its tribulations as a political and cultural entity.

Preliminary archeological findings have placed knowledge of Iranian pre-history at middle paleolithic times (100,000 years ago). The earliest sedentary cultures date from 18,000–14,000 years ago. The sixth millenium B.C. had a fairly sophisticated agricultural society and the beginnings of proto-urban concentrations.

Many dynasties have ruled Iran. Its first period of greatness was under the Acheamenians (559–330 B.C.), a dynasty founded by Cyrus the Great. After the Hellenistic period (300–250 B.C.) came the Parthian (250 B.C.–A.D. 226) and the Sassanian (A.D. 226–651). The Arab Muslim conquest of Iran was followed by the conquests of the Seljuk Turks, the Mongols, and Tamerlane. Iran underwent a revival under the Safavid Dynasty (1501–1736), the most prominent figure of which was Shah Abbas. After the Conqueror Nadir Shah and his successors came the Qajar Dynasty (1795–1925) and the Pahlavi Dynasty (1925–1979).

U.S. Department of State Bureau of Public Affairs, "Iraq," *Background Notes*, December, 1984 and "Iran," *Background Notes*, May, 1982.

Modern Iranian history began with a nationalist uprising in 1905, the granting of a limited constitution in 1906, and the discovery of oil in 1908. In 1921, Reza Khan, an Iranian officer of the Persian Cossack Brigade, seized control of the government. In 1925, he became shah and ruled as Reza Shah Pahlavi for almost 16 years. During his reign, Iran began to modernize, and the central government reasserted its authority over the tribes and provinces. In September 1941, Reza Shah was forced to abdicate in favor of his son, Mohammad Reza Pahlavi.

During World War II, Iran was a vital link in the Allied supply line for lend-lease supplies to the Soviet Union. After the war, Soviet troops stationed in northwestern Iran not only refused to withdraw but backed Communist revolts which established short-lived, pro-Soviet separatist regimes in the northern regions of Azerbaijan and Kurdistan. However, these crumbled in 1946 as a result of U.S. support for Iranian policies and U.S. and U.N. pressure.

The ensuing period witnessed a growth in Iranian nationalism leading to the nationalization of the British-owned oil industry in 1951 under the premiership of Muhammed Mossadeq. Following an abortive coup in August 1953, Mossadeq was arrested by loyalist army forces. The Shah then assumed a more authoritarian role. In 1961, Iran initiated a series of economic, social, and administrative reforms which were formalized in a national referendum in 1963 and came to be known as the Shah's White Revolution. The core of this program was land reform. Modernization and economic growth proceeded at an unprecedented rate. Iran's development program was fueled by its vast petroleum reserves, estimated at 60 billion barrels, third largest in the world, and generating 70% of Iran's revenues.

In 1978, a domestic turmoil swept the country as a result of religious and political opposition to the Shah's rule and programs. Opponents were particularly critical of Western influences on these programs, which did not conform to a fundamentalist interpretation of Shi'a Islam. In January, 1979, the Shah, after appointing a fourth prime minister in less than a year, departed Iran for Egypt. In February 1979, exiled religious leader Ayatollah Khomeini returned from France to direct a revolution resulting in a new, theocratic republic guided by Islamic principles as interpreted by Khomeini.

10

The Islamic government, under Khomeini's autocratic rule, has been characterized by indiscriminate arrests and executions of opponents, economic disorder, and continual crises. These crises included the seizure of the U.S. Embassy compound and its occupants on November 4, 1979 by Iranian militants, an undeclared war with Iraq, continuing power struggles, and internal unrest—all of which have contributed to tension in the region....

Iraq

Once known as Mesopotamia, Iraq was the site of flourishing ancient civilizations, including the Sumerian, Babylonian, and Parthian cultures. The Muslims conquered Iraq in the seventh century A.D. In the eighth century, the Abassid caliphate established its capital at Baghdad, which became a famous center of learning and the arts. By 1638, Baghdad had become a frontier outpost of the Ottoman Empire.

Iraq became a British-mandated territory at the end of World War I. When Iraq was declared independent in 1932, the Hashemite family, which also ruled in Jordan, ruled as a constitutional monarchy. In 1945, Iraq joined the United Nations and became a founding member of the Arab League. In 1955, the Baghdad Pact allied Iraq, Turkey, Iran, Pakistan and the United Kingdom, and established its headquarters in the Iraqi capital.

Gen. Abdul Karim Qasim took power in the coup of July 14, 1958, during which King Faysal and Prime Minister Nuri as-Said were killed. Qasim ended Iraq's membership in the Baghdad pact (later reconstituted as the Central Treaty Organization—CENTO) in 1959. Qasim was assassinated in February 1963, when the Arab Socialist Renaissance Party (Ba'ath Party) took power under the leadership of Gen. Ahmad Hasan al-Bakr as prime minister and Col. Abdul Salam Arif as president.

Arif led a coup ousting the Ba'ath government 9 months later. In April 1966, Arif was killed in a plane crash and was succeeded by his brother, Gen. Abdul Rahman Mohammed Arif. On July 17, 1968, a group of Ba'athists and military elements overthrew the Arif regime. Ahmad Hasan al-Bakr became President of Iraq and Chairman of the Revolutionary Command Council (RCC). In July 1979, al-Bakr resigned and his chosen successor, Saddam Hussein, assumed both offices.

PAST AND PRESENT

MODERN DAY IRAN:
A PROFILE

Joanne Reppert Reams

Geography

Area: 1,648,000 sq. km. (636,294 sq. mi.); slightly larger than
Alaska. **Cities:** *Capital*—Tehran (pop. 5—6 million, est.).
Other cities—Isfahan, Tabriz, Mashad, Shriaz. **Terrain:** Desert
and mountains. **Climate:** Semi-arid; subtropical along Caspian coast.

Physical environment has played a major role in shaping
Iran's destiny. Scarcity and inaccessibility of water, irregular
terrain, and climatic extremes have restricted habitation
generally to the western and most northern parts of the
country. The heaviest concentrations are along the Caspian
coast, in metropolitan Tehran, and in the provinces of East
and West Azerbaijan. About 70% of the country is virtually
uninhabited. The environment has made land development
difficult, time consuming, and expensive.

About one–fifth the size of the United States, Iran is in the
highlands of southwestern Asia....

Joanne Reppert Reams, U.S. Department of State, "Iran,"
Background Notes, May, 1982.

© 1986 Ron Swanson

People

Nationality: *Noun and adjective*—Iranian(s). **Population** (1980 est.): 38.1 million. **Annual growth rate:** 3%. **Ethnic groups:** Persian 63%, Kurds 3%, Arabs 3%, Turkomans and Baluchis 19%, and Lur, Bakhtiari, and Qashqai tribes. **Religions:** Shi'a Muslim 93%; Sunni Muslim 5%; small minorities of Jews; Christians, including Armenians and Assyrians; Bahais; Zoroastrians. **Languages:** Farsi (Persian), Turkish dialects, Kurdish, Arabic, French, English. **Literacy:** 48% (1980 est.). **Health:** *Child death rate*—14/1,000. *Life expectancy*—54 yrs. **Work force** (1979 est.): *Agriculture*—40%. *Industry and commerce*—33%. *Services*—27%....

Two-thirds of Iran's people are of Aryan origin; their ancestors migrated from Central Asia. The major groups in this category include the Persians, Gilani, Mazandarani, Kurds, Lurs, Bakhtiari, and Baluchi. The other third of the population is primarily Turkic, and also includes Arabs, Armenians, Jews, and Assyrians.

Iranian society is divided into urban, market-town, village, and tribal groups. The urban society reflects the upper, middle, and lower classes, while the market-town combines characteristics of both urban and rural environments. About

13

3 million Iranians remain in tribally organized societies and have been least affected by change and social reform.

The urban upper class includes the large landowners, religious leaders, and leaders of the larger tribal federations. The urban middle class is composed of those who have not attained economic or social standing of the elite. Also in this class, but on a lower social level, are groups such as small retailers, artisans, and low-level government employees. There is a substantial gap between the middle and lower classes, the latter ranging from migrants and casual laborers at the bottom to the employed factory and government workers at the top. The class structure, however, should change radically under the new Islamic leadership, staunchly opposed to accumulated wealth.

The market-town is a village of a few thousand inhabitants on a main route, serving as a geographical, economic, and social link between rural and urban areas. The tribal society consists mostly of nomadic and seminomadic herders who inhabit the mountainous rims surrounding the central plateau. The tribe is headed by a hereditary chief and is based more on kinship and traditional criteria than is any other grouping in Iranian society.

Most Iranians are Muslims. Ninety-three percent of the population belong to the Shi'a branch of Islam, the official state religion. About 6% (mainly Kurds and Turks) belong to the Sunni branch of Islam, which predominates in neighboring Muslim countries. Non-Muslim minorities include Zoroastrians, Jews, Bahais, and Christians....

Government

The December 1979 Iranian Constitution defines the political, economic, and social order of the Islamic Republic and grants broad powers to the Muslim clergy. Leadership of the Republic is entrusted to a religious leader (currently Ayatollah Khomeini) or, in the absence of a single leader, to a council of religious leaders. The leader or members of the council of leaders are supposed to emerge from the clerical establishment on the basis of their qualifications and the high esteem in which they are held by Iran's Muslim population.

The leader or council appoints the Council of Guardians, composed of six religious persons and six lawyers; appoints the highest judicial authorities, who must be religious jurists; commands the armed forces; and approves the competence of candidates for the presidency of the republic....

Ayatollah Ruhollah Khomeini, who returned to Iran on February 1, 1979 after 15 years in exile in Turkey, Iraq, and France, is Iran's spiritual and revolutionary leader. Although he holds no political office—he has rejected an official political role in the revolution for himself and his family—Khomeini's approval is required on virtually all government actions and policies.

The Islamic Republican Party (IRP) is Iran's dominant political force. One of its co-founders, Ali Khamenei, serves as Iran's president. Through its members, the IRP controls nearly all branches of the executive, legislative, and judicial structure....

Economy

The current Iranian government appears to favor small-scale trading, farming, and manufacturing. Ruling clerical and lay politicians assert that Iran must free itself from dependence on the outside world and eliminate trading relationships that foster economic dependence. Although Islam guarantees the right to private ownership, banks, insurance companies, and the property of certain individuals have been nationalized. The oil and gas, transportation, utilities, mining, metallurgical, and certain construction sectors have been subjected to interference in various forms. Despite emphasis upon small factories where small producers and consumers determine needs, the Iranian Government's plans and actions suggest increasing government interference in the economy, possibly including the nationalization of foreign trade.

Iran's economy, already severely depressed as a result of the revolution, has been disrupted further by the war with Iraq. All major business and industrial growth indicators are significantly below prerevolutionary levels. Inflation is reportedly 30%–50% annually. Unemployment is up threefold to 3-4 million workers out of an estimated work force of 12 million. Rationing essential items and commodities has become commonplace, although most basic needs are met. Political infighting prevents the formulation of coherent economic policies, while purges of the civil service have eliminated many qualified personnel. Industry is plagued by poor labor productivity, worker interference in management, a lack of competent technical and managerial personnel, and shortages of raw materials and spare parts. Agriculture suffers from shortages of capital, raw materials, and equipment, and food production has declined....

Foreign Relations

Following the fall of the Shah, Khomeini's revolutionary regime initiated sharp foreign policy changes. Iran withdrew the military forces that the Shah had deployed in Oman. Iran also withdrew from the Central Treaty Organization (CENTO), an action which led to CENTO's demise. In the Middle East, Iran has aligned itself with the radical Arab states of Libya and Syria and with the Palestine Liberation Organization against Israel and Egypt. Iran's regional goals are dominated by the desire to curtail or eliminate superpower influence and to encourage Islamization of governments in the Persian Gulf region, especially where substantial Shi'ite communities exist. All revolutionary elements within Iran agree on the broad outline of "Islamic foreign policy," the main points of which include:

- Strict nonalignment;
- Eliminating superpower influence in the region;
- Economic self-sufficiency;
- Xenophobic nationalism; and
- Exporting the Islamic revolution....

In addition to the U.S. hostage crisis, Iran's problems with Iraq escalated into warfare in September 1980. Each regime calls for the overthrow of the other....

For the most part, the Soviet Union has been frustrated in its efforts to improve relations with Iran. The Iranians remain highly suspicious of Soviet intentions toward Iran and critical of Moscow's involvement in Afghanistan....

Limited commercial relations between Iran and the United States continue, mainly in the form of Iranian purchases of food and manufactured products. Continuing Iranian hostility toward the United States and U.S. resentment of the hostage–taking suggest that this trade, and relations between the two countries in general, will not improve in the foreseeable future.

16

PAST AND PRESENT

MODERN DAY IRAQ:
A PROFILE

Juanita Adams

Geography

Area: 434,934 sq. km. (167,924 sq. mi.); about the size of California. **Cities:** *Capital*—Baghdad (pop. 3.8 million). *Other cities*—Basra, Mosul, Kirkuk. **Terrain:** Alluvial plains, mountains, and desert. **Climate:** mostly hot and dry....

Iraq is bordered by Kuwait, Iran, Turkey, Syria, Jordan, and Saudi Arabia. The country slopes from mountains 3,000 meters (10,000 ft.) above sea level along the border with Iran and Turkey to reedy marshes in the southeast. Much of the land is desert or wasteland.

Average temperatures range from higher than 48°C (120°F) in July and August to below freezing in January. Most of the rainfall occurs from December through April and averages between 10 and 18 centimeters (4–7 in.) annually....

People

Nationality: *Noun and adjective*—Iraqi(s). **Population** (1984 est.): 15 million. *Annual growth rate:* 3.3% (1977 census). **Ethnic groups:** Arab (75%), Kurd (15–20%). **Religions:** Shi'a Muslim (55%); Sunni Muslim (40%), Christian (5%). **Languages:** Arabic, Kurdish, Assyrian, Armenian. **Education:** *Years compulsory*—primary school (age 6 through grade 6). *Literacy*—70%. **Health:** *Infant mortality rate*—25/1,000. *Life expectancy*—56.1 years.

Juanita Adams, U.S. Department of State, "Iraq," *Background Notes*, December, 1984.

17

© 1986 Ron Swanson

Iraq's two largest ethnic groups are Arabs and Kurds. Other distinct groups are Assyrians, Turkomans, Iranians, Lurs, and Armenians. Arabic is most commonly spoken. Kurdish is spoken in the North. English is the most commonly spoken Western language.

Iraq is the only Arab country in which a majority of Muslims are members of the Shi'a sect. There are also small communities of Christians, Jews, Bahais, Mandaeans, and Yezidis. Most Kurds are Sunni Muslim but differ from their Arab neighbors in language, dress and customs.

Political Conditions

The Ba'ath Party controls the government. The Kurdish Democratic Party and Kurdish Republican Party nominally participate in a coalition government with the Ba'ath Party under the Popular Progressive National Front, but the Ba'ath Party carefully circumscribes their political activities.

The Iraqi regime does not tolerate opposition. The Communist Party was removed from the coalition and declared illegal in 1979. Since then, its activities have been conducted primarily in exile. The leaders of the outlawed Da'wa (Islamic Call) Party, which seeks to establish an Islamic Republic in Iraq, operate from exile in Iran and other countries.

A large-scale rebellion by elements of the Kurdish population against the Ba'ath government ended in 1975 following the Algiers agreement between Iraq and Iran. The Iraq-Iran conflict has resulted in the renewal of limited anti-regime insurgency in the Kurdish areas of northern Iraq since 1980. The major Kurdish opposition parties are the Kurdish Democratic Party, led by the sons of the late Mustafa Barzani, and the Patriotic Union of Kurdistan of Jalal Talabani. Several senior government officials are Kurds.

Economy

Rising world oil prices since 1973 had sustained expansion in Iraq's gross national product until the Iran-Iraq war. Prewar projections of expenditures on Iraq's 1981-85 economic development plan were as high as $75 billion. Since 1980, increased military imports and reduced export revenues have forced sharp decreases in Iraqi investments in such key infrastructure projects as power and electricity, transportation, and construction. Throughout the 1970's, the government worked toward improving the standard of living by concentrating on education, health, and welfare reforms. Renewed emphasis on these areas is expected upon resolution of the war.

Petroleum

The petroleum sector dominates the Iraqi economy. In 1983, Iraq claimed proven crude oil reserves of 59 billion barrels, third largest in the Organization of Petroleum Exporting Countries (OPEC). Proven reserves of natural gas are 28.8 trillion cubic feet. From late 1979 until mid-September 1980, Iraq produced up to 3.7 million barrels per day (b/d) of petroleum, second highest in OPEC, and consumed about 200,000 b/d. Production capacity has remained virtually intact despite the war, but actual production was cut sharply in late 1980 due to the war's curtailment of Iraq's previously surplus export capacity. War-time production levels have recovered gradually since 1982 to about 1.2 million b/d in 1984. Refining capacity has expanded during the war to exceed 400,000 b/d. Refinery output is probably no higher than 350,000 b/d. With domestic consumption estimated at only 300,000 b/d, in 1983, Iraq was able to begin exporting refined products, primarily fuel oils....

Agriculture

Iraq exports dates but is a large net importer of foodstuffs, principally wheat, rice, and soybean products. Rising consumer demand and the wartime need to reduce imports have increased the importance of raising agricultural output....

Intensive programs are underway to realize the great agricultural potential of Iraq's vast land area and water resources. The government abolished its farm collectivization program in 1981, allowing a greater role for private enterprise in agriculture. The Agricultural Cooperative Bank, capitalized at nearly $1 billion by 1984, has concentrated its low-interest, low-collateral loans to private farmers on mechanization, poultry projects, and orchard development. Large modern cattle, dairy, and poultry farms are under construction....

Trade

The Iran-Iraq war reversed Iraq's foreign trade balance from large surplus into severe deficit, which topped $7 billion in 1982. In 1983, reducing the trade deficit became a primary goal of the Iraqi leadership. Under strict austerity, total Iraqi imports may have fallen as low as $9-10 billion in 1983, or about 50% of the 1982 figure, reducing the 1983 trade deficit to as little as $2-3 billion despite decreased export revenues. By 1984, Iraq's strict austerity program, foreign government subsidies and trade credits, improving oil exports, and foreign supplier's agreements to defer Iraq's payments, had brought relative stability to the Iraqi economy. If Iraq holds imports to current levels and increases oil export revenues through completion of planned pipelines or resolution of the war, its trade balance could return to a surplus within a few years....

Defense

Iraq's war with Iran has caused the Iraqi Government to expand significantly the size of the armed forces and the paramilitary "People's Army" affiliated with the Ba'ath Party. Since the war began in 1980, these forces combined have included more than 500,000 men. As President, Saddam Hussein is commander-in-chief of the Iraqi Armed Forces.

He assumed the rank of field marshal in 1980, following the outbreak of the war.....

Formerly more dependent upon the Soviet bloc for its arms supplies, in the mid-1970's, Iraq began to seek Western suppliers in order to diversify its sources. In recent years, France has become Iraq's leading source of arms after the Soviet Union.

Foreign Relations

Historically difficult Iraqi-Iranian relations had improved following the March 1975 Algiers agreement that ended the Kurdish rebellion and provided for border adjustments. Iraq claims that the Shah never fully implemented the agreement, and it finally welcomed the accession of Iran's revolutionary government in 1979. However, Iranian Shi-ite fundamentalist leader Ayatollah Khomeini, bitter over years of confined exile in Iraq, attempted to incite opposition to Baghdad's secular government. Iraq claimed that its invasion of Iran in September 1980 was in response to a series of border incidents, Iranian-backed assassination attempts, and Iran's failure to honor its 1975 treaty commitments on border adjustments and the Shatt al-Arab waterway. The outbreak of the war stopped all Iraqi shipping and oil exports via the Gulf. From June 1982, when Iraqi forces withdrew from substantially all undisputed Iranian territory, through late 1984, successive bloody engagements on land have not changed the stalemated strategic situation.

Iraq accepted UN Security Council Resolution 540 of October 31, 1983, subject to Iranian acceptance. After Iran rejected this resolution, which called, among other things, for a cease-fire against shipping and ports, Iraq stepped up attacks on Iranian ports and ships serving them. Iran retaliated against ships serving neutral ports. The resulting "tanker war" persisted through 1984. In March 1984, the United States condemned Iraq's use of chemical weapons, which Iraq denied it had used to repulse the "human waves" of Iran's invasion attempt in February of that year. Through summer, Iran threatened another major land offensive, but it had initiated only smaller scale land offensives by the end of 1984.

Iraq has accepted all UN ceasefire resolutions and mediation efforts and other peace initiatives by the Non-aligned Movement, the Organization of the Islamic Conference, and others. Through 1984, the Khomeini regime in Iran continued to reject all such mediation initiatives, demanding the ouster of the Government of Iraq as a precondition for a settlement. Regardless of future changes in regimes or an eventual end of hostilities, ethnic and religious antagonisms probably will persist, and the two countries are likely to maintain their historic rivalry for regional influence....

U.S.-Iraqi Relations

Iraq broke diplomatic relations with the United States during the June 1967 Arab-Israeli war. On November 26, 1984, President Reagan and visiting Iraqi Deputy Prime Minister Tariq Aziz announced the resumption of full diplomatic relations between their two countries. On this date, the U.S. Interests Section in Baghdad, under the Belgian flag since its establishment in 1972, was upgraded to Embassy status. The Iraqi Embassy, which had functioned as an Interests Section under the protection of India, simultaneously was upgraded to Embassy status.

PAST AND PRESENT

HUMAN RIGHTS IN IRAN

U.S. Department of State

Iran

Iran is officially an Islamic Republic under the leadership
of Ayatollah Ruhollah Khomeini. Its formal system, based on
the Constitution approved in 1980 by popular referendum,
follows a parliamentary pattern with a legislature, the Majles,
and a president elected from among multiple candidates by
universal suffrage. However, only candidates meeting highly
restrictive religious and political criteria are permitted to
contest elections, and the choice offered to voters is limited.
The regime's hold on power is reinforced through arrests,
executions, and other forms of intimidation.

The regime is dominated by a political elite composed of a
group of Shi'ite Muslim clerics who support Khomeini and of
laymen aligned with the clerics. The regime, however, is not
monolithic, and there are major differences on theology and
on economic issues such as private property ownership,
government versus private control of foreign trade, industrial
policy, and strategy for the war with Iraq.

The war with Iraq, which began in September 1980, continues with little hope for an end in the near future, given the
Iranian regime's lack of interest in negotiating a settlement.
The war has been costly on both sides. Iran claims that over
100,000 of its soldiers have been killed and that the war has
created about 1 million refugees. Missile and bombing attacks have caused considerable damage to civilian areas and

U.S. Department of State, *Country Reports on Human Rights For
1985,* pp. 1234–36.

23

loss of civilian life. An insurgency in Kurdish areas began about 6 years ago and continues. Urban terrorists cause civilian casualties and property damage in often random bomb attacks.

Nearly 7 years after the 1979 ouster of the Shah and the advent of the Islamic Revolution, the Iranian regime still considers itself revolutionary but must grapple with the need to revive the economy and operate political and social institutions, both old and new, in a productive manner. Iran is an oil-rich developing country. The disruptions of the revolutionary period caused serious economic deterioration. After improving somewhat in the preceding two years, the economy again declined in 1985. Inflation and unemployment are high, and corruption and black market activities flourish.

Although the trend is toward greater adherence to constitutional guarantees of human rights, particularly since December 1982, Iran's human rights record continues to show serious abuses.

Political Killing

Reliable statistics are not available on the number of people killed for political or religious reasons. Due to the lack of procedural safeguards for defendants tried in revolutionary courts, which handle virtually all political cases, most of the hundreds of executions ordered each year by such courts amount to summary executions. It is difficult to separate cases of executions for actual participation in violent activities or narcotics trafficking from cases of executions based purely on the defendant's beliefs, statements, or associations, given the regime's practice of cloaking the latter category with trumped up charges from the former category, but the number of purely political executions in 1985 reportedly includes dozens of persons arrested during demonstrations and summarily executed. At least 6 Baha'is were killed for religious reasons in 1985.

Amnesty International's 1985 annual report recorded an estimated 6,108 executions for all causes in Iran between February 1979 and the end of 1984; the report noted, however, that "Amnesty International believed the true figures were much higher, as former prisoners and relatives

24

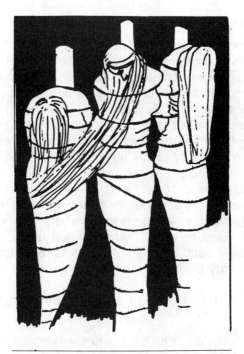

of prisoners consistently testified that large numbers of political prisoners were executed in secret."

Political killings were also perpetrated by opposition groups, including the Mojahedin-e-Khalq, a terrorist organization sometimes known as the People's Mojahedin Organization of Iran. The Mojahedin have claimed responsibility for assassinations with firearms, and dozens of innocent persons, including a four-year-old girl, were killed in 1985 by bombs exploded in public places. The Mojahedin are also believed responsible for bombs delivered, and in some cases exploded, at Iranian diplomatic missions in other countries.

Killings related to the insurrection in the Kurdish area also continue. Although there are no reliable statistics, many deaths have resulted not only from fighting between dissident Kurdish groups and the regime and from regime forces' summary executions of Kurds in captured territory, but also as a result of internecine fighting among Kurdish groups.

Disappearance

Disappearances are seldom permanent in Iran. People are arbitrarily arrested or carried off, they are held without charge, and some are summarily executed; the society, however, is not tightly controlled, so a persistent relative can usually determine who was responsible for the arrest and locate the detainee. Although many relatives are not officially informed of executions, they seem to find out and can often confirm rumor by checking burial records at Tehran's cemetery.

There are, however, some cases of long–term disappearance. One report obtained by Amnesty International stated that sometimes opposition members are listed as "killed while resisting arrest" when in fact they are still alive and in jail. Most such arrests are believed to be the work of the Revolutionary Guard and to be sanctioned by the regime.

Torture and Cruel, Inhuman, or Degrading Treatment or Punishment

Stories of torture in Iran's prisons are rampant and cover a wide range of inhuman practices, particularly in Evin Prison in Tehran, Iran's largest and most notorious. Mock executions are a favorite method of torture there, along with blindfolding and solitary confinement. Beatings of all kinds appear to be common. Prisoners are beaten on the soles of their feet until they can no longer walk. Others have had damaged kidneys as a result of being kicked and beaten.

This torture occurs in government prisons or in government houses in which prisoners of special interest are held for questioning. Presumably it takes place with the sanction of top officials. Many of these reports come from individuals who themselves were in the prisons and who, in some cases, experienced the torture.

The regime continues to revise Iran's civil code to conform more closely with its interpretation of Islamic law. In January the Government announced the development and inauguration of a new machine for surgical amputation of the hands of convicted thieves. As interpreted in Iran, this punishment consists of amputation of the four fingers of the right hand. There were subsequent announcements of the occasional use of this device. Death by stoning reportedly has been

Women in Prison

Dear Friends:

Seven years after the revolution of February 1979, which overthrew the Shah's regime, dictatorship and repression still rule over Iran. By establishing an autocratic rule and reviving the outdated laws and regulations of 1400 years ago under the banner of "Islamic Rule," the Islamic Republic regime is brutally violating the Human Rights Charter, answering the slightest opposition with detention, imprisonment, torture, and execution.

The Islamic regime's notorious prisons are filled with more than 100,000 political prisoners, among whom are thousands of women, young girls of 12-13 years of age and old women. To break the women's spirit of resistance and defiance, and to extract information, the regime's torturers resort to barbaric means! Prolonged interrogations accompanied by beatings and insults, blindfolding for months, solitary confinement, lashing and flogging with leather and metal cables to the point of unconsciousness, burning of the body by cigarettes, insertion of hot needles into the women's breasts, electric shock, hanging by hair, knocking out teeth and pulling out nails, raping women in the presence of their husbands and relatives and the use of narcotics and other psychiatric drugs.

Democratic Organization of Iranian Women
The WREE View of Women, *January, February, 1986*

reinstituted as a punishment for certain crimes against morality, at least in the city of Kerman. There are many reports of floggings, both as a means of torture and as a formal punishment for sexual offenses.

The jails are grossly overcrowded. Toilet facilities are inadequate or totally lacking. Medical treatment is not available, unless the guards believe a prisoner will break and "confess" if enticed by treatment of his wounds. Food is inadequate and sometimes full of dirt and bugs.

In its report, "Torture in the Eighties," Amnesty International expressed concern that torture has become a routine practice in at least some Iranian prisons and noted in particular two kinds of ill-treatment of prisoners: the officially sanctioned punishment of prisoners by whipping, and the torture of prisoners held in incommunicado detention during interrogation to extract confessions.

5 PAST AND PRESENT

HUMAN RIGHTS IN IRAQ

U.S. Department of State

Iraq

Irag is governed by the Arab Ba'ath Socialist Party (ABSP) of Iraq through a Revolutionary Command Council (RCC) which has both executive and legislative authority under the provisional Constitution of 1968. Sadam Hussein holds decisive power as President of the the Republic, Chairman of the Council, and Secretary-General of the Regional Command of the ABSP.

Iraq contains many disparate groups, most notably Shi'a and Sunni Arab Muslims, Kurds, Torcomans, and various Christian sects, predominantly Assyrians and Chaldeans.

In 1985 the war with Iran continued into its sixth year. A major Iranian offensive in March severely tested the Iraqi southern defenses before being defeated. Iran continues to reject Iraqi and international calls for a cease-fire, and to use both military action and terrorism in efforts to overthrow Iraq's secular political system. Tight domestic controls imposed by the Iraqi regime in the name of national security remain in effect, including a decree which prescribes the death penalty for anyone who damages the country's military, political, or economic position. Wartime travel restrictions, which prevent most Iraqi's from departing the country, also remain in force. Iranian prisoners of war (POWs) in Iraq are estimated at approximately 10,000. Most are believed to be registered with the International Committee of the Red Cross (ICRC), which visits the camps. In the

U.S. Department of State, *Country Reports on Human Rights For 1985,* pp. 1246-48.

29

past, POWs in Iraq were believed to have faced instances of physical mistreatment and inadequate diet, but the ICRC reported that treatment in 1985 was improved.

The Ba'ath Party's ideological commitment to increased social, labor, and educational opportunities for women and to the protection of religious minorities continues to be translated into practical action. Iraq has continued to abjure support for terrorist groups and to state its opposition to terrorism. It has said that support for the Palestinian cause does not signify that it condones actions such as the Achille Lauro hijacking. On the other hand, political and individual rights are sharply limited. The news media are subject to censorship. Antiregime activity is dealt with harshly, often by extralegal means employed by a large and feared internal security police force and the intelligence services.

Political Killing

Execution has been an established method for dealing with perceived political and military opponents of the Government, particularly members of the outlawed Da'wa Party (fundamentalist Shi'a Muslim) and the Communist Party. In July 1985 Iraq confirmed to Amnesty International the execution of 16 individuals: 6 members of the banned Kurdistan Democratic Party for committing acts of sabotage, and 10 members of the prominent Hakim family for organizing an opposition political movement and suspected involvement with the Da'wa Party. There have been unconfirmed reports of the execution without trial of three members of the Iraqi Assyrian community for nationalist political activity. Members of the political elite have also been executed as a result of factional conflict, although no such executions are known to have occurred since 1982.

In 1983 and 1985, the military conducted aerial attacks on Kurdish villages suspected of supporting Iranian military incursions into Iraq or harboring antigovernment guerrillas, resulting in unknown numbers of casualties. From time to time there have been reports of executions of military deserters.

After the March 1985 Iranian offensive, Iran renewed charges that Iraq had used chemical weapons, allegations denied by Iraq. In March the State Department spokesman

الحرية للمناضلة عايدة ياسين والمعتقلات العراقيات

FREEDOM TO AIDA YASIN AND
OTHER IRAQI WOMEN DETAINEES

condemned Iraqi use of chemical weapons. Iraq is a party to
the 1925 Geneva Protocol banning use, but not production,
of lethal and incapacitating chemical weapons. There are indications that Iraq continues to stockpile lethal agents....

Disappearance

Iraqi emigrants have reported that some suspects, particularly those detained by the security police for subversion,
disappear following detention. It is difficult in such cases to
ascertain whether the subject has been executed or has died
while incarcerated. In October 1983 Amnesty International
submitted to Iraq the names of 114 people whose
whereabouts remain unknown since their abduction between
1979 and 1982. Subsequent reports from Amnesty International indicate other instances of disappearance, among
which is the alleged disappearance in 1984 of 153 Assyrians.

31

Antigovernment Kurds in Northern Iraq occasionally kidnap foreign workers and businessmen. Ransom demands have included money, a halt to Western economic cooperation with Iraq, and support for the release of prisoners in Iraq. Victims generally have been released following negotiations involving overseas Kurdish representatives, the victim's employers, and Iraqi security organizations.

Torture and Cruel, Inhuman, or Degrading Treatment or Punishment

The Constitution prohibits torture and prescribes stiff punishment for it, and the Government rejects charges that it practices torture. Nevertheless, reliable reports make clear that both physical and psychological torture are used by the authorities, especially the security police. Given the rigid chain of command within the Government and security services, it is unlikely that torture could be practiced without the authorization of senior officials.

According to former prisoners, persons detained by the security police for political or security-related matters are frequently tortured and mistreated. Treatment is reported to be worst immediately following arrest and during the period of interrogation and investigation, which can last for months. Torture and brutal treatment are not limited to political cases. Security-related offenses include such routine criminal matters as currency violations.

The security forces' methods of torture, often to extract confessions or information about the suspect and his colleagues, reportedly include beatings with fists and rubber truncheons, electrical shocks to the genitals and other parts of the body, and the extraction of fingernails and toenails. A. Tunisian, who was detained for 10 months by Iraqi security forces and released in 1984, alleged torture while in custody. Subsequent medical examinations in Paris under the auspices of Amnesty International concluded that the signs of physical and mental trauma were consistent with the allegations.

PAST AND PRESENT

THE IRAN-IRAQ WAR:
AN OVERVIEW

Nancy Greenberg

Now in its sixth year, the Iran–Iraq war is the longest war between two neighboring countries since World War II. The war has resulted in death, injury, or loss of property to millions of Iranians and Iraqis. U.S. military estimates of the dead and wounded over a year ago were as high as 950,000. Threatening the security of all Middle Eastern peoples, the Iran–Iraq war involves Americans because of U.S. overt and covert action in the region. And it is a war that concerns the entire world because of U.S. preparations for military intervention in the Persian Gulf region and the Indian Ocean.

The Human Cost

Nearly every Iraqi and Iranian southern and western city has been hit, creating many civilian casualties. The Iraqi invasion of September 1980 created 1.5 million refugees in only the first few months of the war. Besides the enormous human cost on both sides, economic losses from the war exceed $200 billion *(Iran Today Supplement, Sept. 1985)*. Not only have huge quantities of arms been imported into both countries, making the battlefield a testing ground for new weapons, but agricultural growth has declined in both countries as a result of the war.

Nancy Greenberg, "The Iran–Iraq War," *Peace and Freedom,* July/August, 1985, pp. 18–19.

The Iran-Iraq war slowed the movement for social justice and democratic rights in Iran by forcing the year and a half-old revolutionary government to turn much of its energy toward the military and away from the progressive aims of the popular Iranian revolution. The Islamic Republic consolidated its right-wing power, due in part to the confusion and propaganda related to the war. The democratic movement in Iraq among the Kurds, Shi'ites and Iraqi communists, who together comprise a majority of the population, has also been slowed by the war and the repressive measures taken to enforce the war effort.....

Despite all repressive measures, including arrests, torture, and execution, taken against them, both Iranian and Iraqi progressive movements firmly condemn the war. From the first months of the Iraqi offensive, progressive Iraqis opposed the war, though nationalism increased and Iraqis fought bravely when the Islamic Republic invaded. At the same time, progressive Iranians opposed a continuation of the war. In the spring of 1984, the will of the Iranian people for peace and democratic rights showed renewed signs of life and struggle. In elections held at that time, Iranian people expressed their dissatisfaction with the war, the inflated economy, and the Islamic Republic's opposition to human rights.

U.S. Policy

In its policy toward the war, the Reagan Administration has declared a concern for peace, claimed that our "vital interests" are being threatened in the Persian Gulf, when in fact we are not dependent on the area for oil *(Iran Today Supplement, Sept. 1984),* and threatened to invade the Persian Gulf. Since the 1982 invasion of Iraq, the Reagan Administration has cautiously avoided alienating either the Islamic Republic or Iraq, as the outcome of the war remains uncertain. Primarily through her Western and Middle Eastern allies, the U.S. has supplied both Iran and Iraq with the arms to keep fighting.

As Americans we must support the peace struggle of Iranians and Iraqis. Their peace is our peace.

INTERPRETING EDITORIAL CARTOONS

This activity may be used as an individualized study guide for students in libraries and resource centers or as a discussion catalyst in small group and classroom discussions.

Although cartoons are usually humorous, the main intent of most political cartoonists is not to entertain. Cartoons express serious social comment about important issues. Using graphic and visual arts, the cartoonist expresses opinions and attitudes. By employing an entertaining and often light-hearted visual format, cartoonists may have as much or more impact on national and world issues as editorial and syndicated columnists.

Points to Consider

1. Examine the two cartoons in this activity.

2. How would you describe the message of each cartoon? Try to describe each message in one to three sentences.

3. Do you agree with the message expressed in either cartoon? Why or why not?

4. Do either of the cartoons support the author's point of view in any of the readings in this publication? If the answer is yes, be specific about which reading or readings and why.

5. Are any of the readings in chapter one in basic agreement with either of the cartoons?

Reprinted with permission of the *Minneapolis Star and Tribune*

CHAPTER 2

ORIGINS OF THE WAR

7 ORIGINS OF THE WAR

THE IRANIAN REVOLUTION

Library of Congress

Iran's present troubles have their roots in the unresolved issues of the past: a fear and distrust of foreigners, and the continuing debate over the correct path for Iran, secular or temporal, traditional or modern, constitutional democracy or absolute monarchy.

Reza Khan's reign as Shah of Iran (1925-1941) was marked by his attempts to rid the nation of foreigners and foreign influence and to institute reforms needed to modernize the country. In each enterprise he was only moderately successful. Iran curtailed but did not eliminate the influence of British, Germans, and Russians because their expertise and capital were needed. Reza dictated some reforms in education, communication, transportation, women's rights, and other areas, but compromised others for the sake of maintaining a peaceful balance among the divergent elements of the society. Perhaps the most interesting compromise accepted by the new Shah in 1925 was to forego his intention to turn Iran into a republic because Iran's religious leaders feared that democracy would destroy the traditional way of life.

In 1941, Britain invaded Iran because it suspected the Shah's neutralism was too pro-German, and forced Reza Khan to abdicate in favor of his 22 year-old son, Muhammad Reza Pahlavi. At the end of World War II, Britain and the United States ended their occupation of Iran, but the Soviet

Excerpted from *The Iran-Iraq War,* Library of Congress Pamphlet, Foreign Affairs Division, September, 1979.

Union remained, agreeing to withdraw only in exchange for an oil concession in the north of Iran. A Soviet-Iranian oil agreement was signed in 1946, the Soviet forces withdrew, but the Majlis (parliament) rejected the agreement. A new British-Iranian oil agreement in 1949, despite its benefits to Iran,triggered a revival of anti-foreign nationalism, which culminated in the April 1951 law nationalizing the oil industry.

The populist leader of the nationalization movement, Muhammad Mussadiq, became Prime Minister in May 1951, but dissension among his supporters, a widening rift with the Shah, and the near financial collapse of Iran brought on by the street disturbances and the closure of the oil industry, led to a coup d'etat in August 1953. General Zahedi restored order, returned the Shah to the Throne (he had left Iran prior to the coup), and opened negotiations with the Americans and the British for a restoration of the oil industry. Oil began flowing after a new agreement was signed in September 1954. The military government resigned in April 1955, and was replaced by a civilian government.

Continuing economic problems plus opposition political party charges of irregularities in Iran's first election in August 1960 led to another series of public disturbances. The National Front (a coalition of opposition forces legalized in 1958) complained that a second election held in January 1961 was also fraudulent. In May 1961, the Shah appointed Ali Amini, a National Front leader, to be Prime Minister. Amini introduced a series of reforms (balanced budget, anti-corruption campaign, land reform, civil service, etc) but resigned in July 1962 after more riots and strikes, which were triggered by the announcement that elections scheduled for July would be postponed. A new government led by Assadollah Alam, a supporter of the Shah, held a referendum in January 1963 to approve a reform program which became the basis for the Shah's "White Revolution."

Succeeding governments until 1975 supported the Shah. In 1975, the Shah declared opposition parties illegal, and regrouped the nation's political parties under the Rastakhiz (resurgence) Party. This muzzling of the opposition added to the growing dissatisfaction with the pace of modernization and the economic dislocations caused by rapid industrialization, a resurgence of religious feelings, a questioning of the

Funeral Procession

role of traditional values in a modern society, a disenchant-
ment with the increasing numbers of foreigners in Iran, and
resentment over the harsh repressive measures of SAVAK,
the state secret police, provided the basis for the demonstrations, protests, strikes, and riots of 1978.

Iranian Society and Opposition to the Shah

Iran is not a homogeneous nation. Some 65% of Iran's
citizens speak Farsi and are racially Iranian (Aryan), or are
related to Iranians, such as the Bakhtiari, Lurs, Kurds,
Baluchis, or the Gilani. Another 25% are Turkic in race and
language, such as the Azaris, Turkomans, or Qashqai. The
remaining 10% are primarily Arabs, with a scattering of
Armenians, Jews, Assyrians, and others. Most Iranians are
Muslim (93% Shiah, 5% Sunni), with the remainder being

41

Christians, (Armenians and Assyrians), Jews, Bahais, and Zoroastrians. About 10% of the population is nomadic, mainly the Bakhtiari, Qashqai, Baluchis, and some of the Turkomans. 45% of Iran's 35 million people are urban dwellers.

Religion

Islam means submission to the will of God: those who submit are Muslims. God instructed a series of prophets (Adam, Abraham, Moses, Solomon, and Jesus, among others) to guide mankind on the correct way of life, but eventually mankind deviated from the "straight path" taught by these prophets. Finally, God, speaking through the angel Gabriel, dictated to Muhammad, the last of the prophets, the ultimate guide for life, the Quran [also spelled Koran]. Armed with the Quran and the "Hadith," the recorded sayings and actions of Muhammad, the early Muslims spread Islam over the Middle East, North Africa, Central Asia, and reached into Europe, China, and India. But a schism developed soon after Muhammad's death in 622 A.D. between those who followed the community's elected leaders—the Sunnis—and those who believed Muhammad appointed his cousin and son-in-law Ali as his successor—the Shiah [Shi'a]. Shiites believe Muhammad was divinely inspired, and that the divine inspiration was passed on to Ali and his heirs (the Imams, or religious leaders, whose number is in dispute). Iran's Shiah Muslims today are less inclined to follow the Hadith and more inclined to accept liberal or independent interpretations of the Quran, to lean toward asceticism and mysticism, and to follow the guidance of the ulama (religious leaders). Shiah Islam, with its heirarchy of Mullahs (local religious leaders), Mujtahids (religious scholars), and Ayatollahs (elder religious divines), seems suited to Iran's 3,000-year-old tradition of a strong monarch allied to the influential priestly class. But the alliance was shattered by Reza Khan's reforms, such as his support of women's rights, and by Muhammad Reza's land reform, which distributed church lands to the peasants.

In recent years, the religious community, led by the Mullahs, Mujtahids, and Ayatollahs, and encompassing a cross-section of classes in Iran from the peasants to the elite, became active in the protests against the Shah. In most Islamic countries, religion is a pervasive force in the society, touching every aspect of daily life. Emphasizing religious values may be a way of combatting the confusion arising from the transition from an ancient to a modern society. Islam provides simple, direct, and proven answers for problems of daily life, and appeals to people who are comfortable with their traditions but not with interest rates, union contracts, cost–benefit ratios, development infrastructure, cost overruns, and other complexities of modern industrial societies. Religious leaders and their followers attacked the Shah as the leader of the modernization movement and as the one most responsible for the problems that have resulted from it.

Class Elements in Iran

An important element in Iranian society is the *elite class,* the wealthy land owners, intelligencia,military leaders, politicians and diplomats, and religious leaders who are Iran's "establishment." The reform movements of 1906, 1925, 1953, and the Shah's "White Revolution" of 1963 curtailed, but did not end, their power and prestige by redistributing land to the peasants, opening the political process to the peasants and workers, and providing opportunities through industrialization and education for the emergence of a middle class. For the most part, the elite continued to support the monarchy and the Shah despite its decline in power. The exception was the ulama, who became a force in opposition to the Shah after the Shah stripped away most of the religious community's land....

The peasant and working classes were beneficiaries of land reform, the "literacy corps," and "health corps," employment opportunities arising from industrialization and democratization. But they were also the victims of inflation, unfulfilled political expectations, surveillance by the secret police, and the severe social, cultural, and economic dislocations that resulted from urbanization and modernization....

Students, young technocrats, and a sizeable segment of the middle class, many of whom were educated abroad and are more worldy than the peasants and farmers, favor democratic, economic, and social reforms that will limit or eliminate what they view as the dictatorial power of the Shah and the elite, and will liberalize or open society. Many favor socialism over capitalism, because capitalism, in their view, supports the elite and does not benefit the lower classes. Their view of the religious heirarchy is ambivalent, favoring the religious community's call for a return to traditional values and rejection of foreigners but at the same time opposing the Mullah's demands for a return to rigid Islamic law. The middle class is the most changeable element in the group because they enjoy some of the privileges of the elite, which they would like to protect, but at the same time believe that they have been cheated by the elite out of their share of the industrialization wealth.

Political Parties

Traditionally, most political parties in Iran coalesced around broad ideological bases rather than specific programs, had charismatic leaders, and did not have large, loyal following among the people. The Rastakhiz was a coalition of factions supporting the Shah's "White Revolution" and industrialization program, and from 1975 to 1979 had been the legal political party of Iran. The primary opposition party was the National Front, a coalition of political factions opposing the Shah's autocratic determination of what was best for Iran. The National Front first appeared in the 1950's during the oil nationalization crises, but faded after the Shah's 1963 reform program. It was revived in December 1977 when the opposition to the Shah became widespread. The Tudeh party (literally, "Masses") was a Soviet-inspired communist party of the 1940's that moved away from Moscow in the 1950's and has been underground and illegal since the coup of 1953.

The Rastakhiz disappeared with the Shah's removal in February 1979. A loose coalition of leftists, socialists, and Communists, led by the Cherikha-ya Fadaye Khalg (People's sacrifice guerillas) emerged in opposition to the religious-right Khomaini supporters, led by the Guardians of the Revolution. Between these right and left blocs were holdovers of the old political factions, a few monarchists, advocates of a centralized republican government to replace the Khomaini-led group, ethnic political groups such as the Kurds, Turkomans, and Arabs, and some special interest groups such as women.

Popular Opposition

A wave of popular opposition to the Shah began building after the 1975 formation of the Rastakhiz and the banning of opposition political parties . About the same time, it became clear that the increased oil revenues following the 1974 oil price increases were to be spent on arms and large industrialization projects. Early in 1977, students calling for reforms and more rapid modernization began attacking the Shah. In mid-1977, the religious leaders began demonstrating against the modernization and the new wave of foreign technicians. In November 1977, several people were killed when police broke up demonstrations and strikes. Mourning services traditionally held 40 days after death became the occasions for the next demonstration, which led to more deaths—a pattern that continued throughout most of 1978. In the spring of 1978, dissident groups joined forces—cautiously at first—to attack the Shah: workers seeking higher wages, peasants and the middle class opposing higher wages and inflation, farmers seeking agrarian reform programs, businessmen seeking industrialization, religious leaders opposed to industrialization and modernization, students seeking more modernization, socialists denouncing capitalism, capitalists denouncing communism-each group focusing its attack on the Shah, but for different reasons....

Many observers believed that the military government would stop the demonstrations by force, and that the crisis in Iran was at an end. The test came in early December, during Muharram, a 10-day period of religious processions to commemorate the deaths of Shiah martyrs Hassan and Hussayn, Ali's sons. The military was confronted with the choice of stopping all demonstrations and risk being branded as anti-religious, or allowing the demonstrations to continue and perhaps become more serious. The military allowed the demonstrations to continue through Muharram. It appeared that the Shah, his supporters, and particularly the military, had lost the will to fight the demonstrators.

It was also evident that the protests had become almost wholly religious in appearance, that other complaints of the demonstrators had been submerged under the rubric of religion. The change was due in large measure to the

Ayatollah Ruhallah Khomaini. For speaking out against the Shah's autocratic rule, Khomaini was exiled to Turkey in 1963. In 1965, Khomaini moved to Iraq where he became the central spokesman for expatriat opposition to the Shah. On Oct. 6, 1978, Khomaini was expelled from Iraq and moved to Paris, where he was accessible to a larger body of expatriat opposition forces, and, perhaps just as important, to the Western press. Khomaini became the spokesman and symbol of the opposition to the Shah. Ayatollah Khomaini claims he will be the guide for the Islamic republic that displaced the Shah, and will expell the foreigners, enforce religious and traditional values, and redirect Iran's wealth away from large industrialization schemes and toward reforms needed by the common people....

After a year of public demonstrations against him, the Shah of Iran left Teheran on Jan. 16, 1979, for an "extended vacation," leaving the country in the hands of a regency council and Prime Minister Shahpur Bakhtiar, for years a member of the National Front opposition to the Shah. Iranian military leaders offered their support to Bakhtiar because their commander-in-chief, the Shah, had told them to do so. A variegated array of demonstrators seeking political and economic reforms, an end to the monarchy, expulsion of foreigners, modernization, and a return to traditional values, rallied around Ayatollah Ruhallah Khomaini and his call to replace the Shah and Bakhtiar with an Islamic Republic. Khomaini, after 15 years in exile in Iraq and Paris, returned to Iran on Feb. 1, 1979, to tumultuous welcome. On Feb. 11, Bakhtiar resigned along with the parliament, and Mehdi Bazargan, the Khomaini-appointed Prime Minister, took over the government.

8 ORIGINS OF THE WAR

HISTORICAL BACKGROUND

U.S. Foreign Relations Committee

The current fighting between Iraq and Iran has its historical roots in the cultural differences between Arabs and Persians. For centuries, Arabs have fought Persians, and Ottomans have fought Persian Sassanids in this very region. Not long after the current war began, President Saddam Hussein constructed a large panorama commemorating the battle of Qadisiya, fought in 637, in which the Arab Islamic armies defeated the Persian Empire and established Islam as the religion of Iran. In Iraq, the war is now often called Saddam's Qadisiya.

Over the centuries, the border has shifted back and forth as one side gained strength and the other weakened. By the middle of the 17th century, the border was roughly at its current position. The most important issue was over who controlled the Shatt-al-Arab which rises at the confluence of the Tigris and Euphrates rivers and flows 120 miles to the Persian Gulf, providing Iraq with its primary access to the sea. In 1847, Great Britain and Russia attempted to delineate the border between the Ottoman and Persian Empires, but their efforts floundered over the issue of control of the Shatt. In 1913, under British pressure, Iran reluctantly recognized Ottoman sovereignty over it. The Iranians never truly reconciled themselves to the decision that their shore and not the Thalweg (the middle of the river channel) was the border. Under Iranian pressure, the Iraqis recognized the Thalweg principle only opposite the Iranian ports of Abadan and Khorramshahr.

Excerpted from *War In The Gulf,* a staff report prepared for the Senate Foreign Relations Committee, August, 1984, pp. 5-7.

Increased Tensions

Tensions between pro-Soviet Baaths in Iraq and pro-American imperial Iran again increased in the late 1960s and early 1970s. The border again was a primary source of contention. As the balance of power shifted in favor of American-armed and supported Iran, pressures were exerted on Iraq to accept border modifications. Each side supported dissident elements in the other, and minor border clashes between the two armies were not uncommon. The simmering conflict between Islamic neighbors and fellow members of OPEC was disturbing to other Muslim oil exporting nations. At the 1975 OPEC meeting in Algiers, under Algerian auspices, Iran and Iraq reached agreement settling their dispute.

Iraq recognized the Thalweg of the Shatt as the border. Both agreed to stop interfering in the internal affairs of the other. Iran terminated support for the Iraqi Kurds and their rebellion was effectively ended. Iran also agreed to give Iraq several small pieces of disputed territory located in their central border region. Although these pieces of territory were never returned, both sides believed the agreement relieved regional tensions. When the Shah in 1978 asked the Baathi regime in Baghdad to expel Iranian dissident Ayatollah Khomeini, the Iraqis agreed, not wanting to undermine stable relations with the Shah. Khomeini's expulsion after 15 years of exile in socialist Iraq seemed to be the basis of his enmity toward that regime and its leader.

After the Shah was deposed early in 1979, tensions between the two states again increased. Ayatollah Khomeini called on Iraqi Shia, who formed a majority of the population, to overthrow the secular Baathi government. The Iranians also supported dissident elements, including the Iraq Dawa Party, which conducted terrorist attacks throughout Iraq. Ayatollah Khomeini left little doubt that he would not be satisfied until an Islamic Republic was established in Iraq under the rule of the Shia majority.

The Iraqis did not welcome the Islamic revolution in Iran. A strong stable neighbor was transformed into a radical force determined to divide Iraq along religious lines. The possibility of an Islamic Iraq was anathema to secular Iraqi leaders.

48

Missile Attack on Abadan

Following the revolution, the Iranian Government faced revolts in Azerbaijan, Iranian Kurdistan, Baluchistan and elsewhere. These disturbances offered Baghdad an opportunity to weaken its neighbor by supporting dissidents. Among those being supported were the Arabs in the province of Khuzistan. Baghdad's fear was that once the Ayatollah suppressed domestic opposition, Iraq would be directly threatened. These fears were enhanced by a series of border incidents.

Iraqi Invasion

Through a series of miscalculations, the Iraqis launched a pre-emptive strike in September 1980. They apparently believed that the local Arabs in Khuzistan, historically an Arab-dominated region, would rise in support of invading Iraqis, the Iranian army would crack, and the government in Tehran would either collapse or agree to a ceasefire. None of this occurred. Despite significant Iraqi advances, the Iranian army continued to perform. The local Arab population did not rise up. Moreover, the Iraqi invasion helped the Iranian regime solidify its position. The Iranians launched attacks on key Iraqi economic facilities destroying its primary oil export facilities at Fao and damaging other installations, including power generating plants. Despite the advance of Iraqi troops through more than half of Khuzistan and an offer to negotiate a settlement, Iran would not yield. Arguing that they were the aggrieved party, the Iranians insisted on the liberation of all their territory and the removal of the Baathi regime in Baghdad.

A succession of Iranian counterattacks began in September 1981 forcing the Iraqis to retreat from much territory they occupied during the previous year. The Iranian successes underlined the reinvigoration of the Iranian armed forces, greater Iranian manpower, and better coordination between the regular army and the Revolutionary Guard. Following the Israeli invasion of Lebanon in June 1982, Iraq announced its willingness to end hostilities between the two Islamic states. Moreover, the Iraqis (1) stated their intention to withdraw from all Iranian territory that it still occupied within 2 weeks and (2) declared their willingness to accept binding arbitration by the Islamic Conference. Iran rejected

50

the offer as "too late" and not providing for the removal of President Saddam Hussein. The Iraqis, nevertheless, withdrew forces from Iran in an apparent effort to gain the moral high ground and in recognition that the Iranians could probably capture this territory anyway.

In July 1982, the Iranians began attacking Iraqi territory. During the past 2 years, Iraqi forces have been primarily defending their own territory while inflicting heavy losses on attacking Iranians. Some very minor advantages have been gained by Iran, but at a tremendous cost in lives and equipment. Both parties have demonstrated that they will pay high costs and use whatever means necessary to win a victory. The Iraqis have used chemical weapons while the Iranians have marched young volunteers across minefields.

Iraq appears to have adopted its defensive strategy out of necessity and a desire to preserve its more limited human resources. The Iraqis apparently hope to hold their defensive position while bringing international pressure to bear on Iran to agree to a settlement. Their strategy seems to be to convince the international community to put economic pressure on Iran and to prevent Iran from resupplying its depleted military stores. For their part, the Iranians still consider themselves the aggrieved party deserving of retribution. Until recently, no one in Iran appeared to be considering anything short of a clear military victory. Over the past few months, however, some in the leadership of Iran appear to be having second thoughts about continuing the war.

9 ORIGINS OF THE WAR

THE MILITARY CONFLICT

Richard M. Preece

War of Attrition

To date, the Iran–Iraq war has become a war of attrition—a static conflict since mid-1982 in which the line of battle has not moved more than a few miles from the common border. The pattern of operations in general has become one of periodic Iranian offenses, launched partly in the hope of breaking through Iraqi lines and partly to wear down the Iraqi forces. Tactically, the Iranians have persisted in attacking, using massed infantry, but battles have not been fought to decisive conclusions, in large measure because the Iranians have lacked the equipment and spare parts, firepower, and logistic support to achieve effectively their objectives or to exploit breakthroughs. Neither side has made use of weapons essential for a war of maneuver.

Since June 9, 1985, Iranian ground operations have taken the form of rapid, small-scale attacks against the Iraqi lines in all three sectors of the 780-mile front. Majlis Speaker Rafsanjani stated at the time that Iran's intent was "to achieve victory with as few casualties as possible;" and Pasdaran Chief of Staff Ali Reza Afshur asserted on June 23 that Khomeini has issued "an overall order for a defensive holy war."

In early February 1986, Iraqi units repulsed Iranian attacks in the marshlands north of Basra. On Feb. 10, Iranian forces crossed the Shatt-al-Arab southeast of Basra and succeeded in occupying the Iraqi port of Al-Faw. Tehran increased

Richard M. Preece, *The Iran–Iraq War,* Library of Congress pamphlet, Foreign Affairs Division, March, 1986.

pressure on Iraq by opening an attack on Feb. 24 in the northern sector, in conjunction with dissident Iraqi Kurds and exiled Shiite units. Iran claimed in early March to have advanced to within 25 km. of Sulaymaniya. The apparent objective was to tie down Iraqi forces in the northern and southern extremities of the front, thereby making Iraq more vulnerable to a full-scale offensive north of Basra. U.S. officials were reported to have found Iraq's inability to dislodge the Iranians from the Al-Faw Peninsula "disturbing" in that this was the first time that Iran held territory undisputably Iraqi.

A number of observers consider that the Iranian leadership, armed with knowledge that it cannot lose the war militarily and having conditioned its economy, its people and its foreign policy to the concept of a prolonged conflict, has decided to continue the war of attrition in order to bring down the Iraqi regime of Saddam Hussein. While the war has impinged strongly on Iranian national life and casualties have been heavy, fighting has taken place at a distance from the principal cities. The stepping up of Iraqi air attacks on population centers in early 1985, including Tehran, reportedly has succeeded in prompting some limited anti-war demonstrations within Iran. (To date, Iraq has not used its Soviet-supplied SS-12 (SCALEBOARD) surface-to-surface missiles, with a range of 450-500 miles, that reportedly it had taken delivery in January 1984.) It should be noted that Iraqi Foreign Minister Aziz in June 1984 had cited some 80 potential strategic targets in Iran, including oil refineries at the principal cities and the Qotor bridge, the destruction of which would cut Iran's rail link with Turkey.

Iran continues to finance its war effort through petroleum exports which have ranged between 1.6 million and 2.1 million barrels per day except for periodic drops as a result of Iraqi air attacks against tankers in the northern Gulf. Tehran continues to reject all attempts at mediation and negotiations for a settlement of the conflict. Iraq, on the other hand, has faced economic difficulties with its primary oil export terminals having been destroyed early in the war, its trans-Syrian pipeline cut off because of Syria's support for Iran and its hostility toward the Baghdad regime, and its remaining pipeline through Turkey facilitating some 1 million barrels per day. Since September 1985, between 300,000 and

500,000 b/d is trucked to Agaba, Jordan, and through Turkey. With a population of only a third of its adversary, Iraq faces greater difficulties than Iran in sustaining the heavy casualties of a war of attrition, and it has expressed its willingness to join mediation efforts to end the conflict.

The Air War in the Gulf

Since August 1982, when Iraqi President Hussein declared a maritime exclusion zone in the northern Gulf, the Iraqi air force has been increasingly active in attacking shipping and offshore oil installations in that zone.

Iraq's objectives are to prevent or reduce the importation of vital materials required by Iran for its war effort and to reduce or terminate Iran's financial means to conduct war through its oil exports. It should be noted that until Mar. 27, 1984, Iraq had refrained from striking the Kharg Island Terminal, which handles some 90% of Iran's oil exports. In addition, despite its numerical air superiority, Iraq had not attempted to destroy the Kharg facilities, perhaps because of concentrations of air defense protecting the terminal. Iraqi Foreign Minister Aziz reiterated on May 19 his government's intentions of continuing to interdict shipping to and from Kharg Island and Iran's northern ports, emphasizing Iraq's objective of demonstrating to the Tehran regime that "the elusive war of attrition which they bet on is not in their interest."

The Iranian response in mid-May 1984 by attacking Kuwaiti and Saudi oil tankers outside the exclusion zone near Arab shores appeared to indicate Tehran's signalling to Iraq and its Gulf Arab financial supporters that Iraq's efforts to reduce Iranian oil exports would not go unchallenged, and to prompt the Gulf Arab states to use their influence in urging Baghdad to cease the escalating attacks on Iran-destined shipping. Iranian Majlis Speaker Rafsanjani declared on May 15 that "if the Kharg Island route is not safeguarded, then no other routes in the Persian Gulf will be secure...."

Between mid-1981 and mid-1985, according to Lloyd's Intelligence Services, 141 neutral ships have been sunk or damaged as a result of Iraqi and Iranian air attacks. Overall, however, the air war has had only a slight affect upon deterring the movement of oil and goods in the region. To offset future suspensions of shipments from the Kharg Island ter-

Victim of a Bombing

minal, the Iranian Oil Ministry is loading crude from its Lavan Island terminal (150,000 b/d capacity) and two 500,000-ton tankers anchored off Sirri Island, near the Strait of Hormuz, replenished by shuttle tankers from Kharg. Iran is also moving ahead with plans to construct pipelines that will permit an export capacity of up to 1.5 million b/d from floating terminals or ultra-large crude carriers south of Kharg Island. As of March 1986, Tehran had postponed its decision to proceed with its oil export pipeline scheme.

Mediation Efforts

Since the beginning of the conflict in September 1980, there have been several mediation efforts designed to achieve an end to the war on the part of international and regional organizations as well as individual countries. All such efforts have failed because of Iran's insistence that any resolution to the conflict must contain the following conditions: the unconditional withdrawal of all Iraqi forces from Iranian territory; the convening of an international tribunal to determine the aggressor; the payment of war reparations (placed by Ayatollah Khomeini at $150 billion); the return of some 100,000 Shi'ites expelled by Iraq; and the overthrow of Iraqi President Husayn and his leadership. Many observers consider that a negotiated settlement is unlikely so long as Ayatollah Khomeini, who continues to insist on Iraqi President Husayn's removal from office, retains power. Some analysts, however, point to broadcasts by Khomeini in early June 1984 hinting to Iranian listeners that negotiations might be possible. Majlis leader Rafsanjani in July 1985 commented on the "penalization" rather than the "removal" of the "aggressor"....

Internal Conditions

The Iranian attempts to invade Iraqi territory appear to have muted expressions of discontent within Iraq despite the introduction of austerity programs and the decreased development spending. Internal political opposition, including Shi'ite groups, Syrian-supported Ba'athists, and Kurdish and Communist elements, have not to date posed a serious internal threat to the Baghdad regime. President Husayn, in June 1982, had consolidated his leadership by effecting sweeping changes within both the Ba'ath Party and the Revolution Command Council. Coercive control is efficient. Nevertheless, the regime is confronted with a population that may become increasingly restive because of economic difficulties and casualties on the front.

In Iran, the Khomeini regime appears to face no serious threat for the present. The Iranian government is dependent on oil revenues for 80% of its budget income. Continuing Iraqi air attacks affect the future levels of oil exports. Many observers consider that, in the long term, Iran's economy is strong, given the country's resources, but currently, foreign exchange problems are clearly apparent. Iran is having to barter away about one-third of its sole source of foreign currency to maintain import levels and avoid shortages (particularly foodstuffs). The level of foreign exchange reserves is subject to speculation, with some estimates indicating that, as of February 1986, reserves totalled between $6 billion to $8 billion. Iran has managed virtually to eradicate its foreign debt. The country's economic problems remain unresolved. Little progress has been achieved toward the goal of self-sufficiency. Economic policies are still in the process of formulation and, six years after the revolution, the regime's final economic philosophy has yet to be precisely defined....

Regional Effects of the Conflict

Of particular concern to the United States is the potential of a widening of the conflict that could increase prospects for destabilizing the region and endanger U.S. interests. From the beginning, the Iran–Iraq war created realignments among Arab states and deepened existing cleavages in the Arab world. Indeed, it almost led to armed confrontation between Syria and Jordan in late 1980.

Jordan was the most vociferous Arab state in support of Iraq and that support took a number of forms, including political advocacy, the opening of its port at Aqaba for unloading supplies destined for Iraq, and volunteers to serve alongside Iraqi forces. King Husayn's support for Iraq was seen by some observers as a way of balancing Jordan's financial dependence on Saudi Arabia.

Syria, in contrast, has effectively supported Iran because of its hostility toward the Baghdad regime, reflected in its condemnation of Iraqi military moves against Iran. Syrian motives were interpreted as being another manifestation of the rivalry between the two Ba'athist regimes in Damascus and Baghdad over the leadership of the Ba'ath and Arab world. In addition, the ruling Alawite elite in Damascus are members of a minority sect in Syria that is an offshoot of Shi'ism.

The reaction of other Arab states to the conflict fell between the Jordanian and Syrian positions. The Gulf Arab states lent financial support to Iraq (an estimated $30 billion) in its conduct of the war. Iran repeatedly has countered with strong warnings in efforts to intimidate Gulf countries and, in its Arabic broadcasts, has called for the overthrow of ruling regimes. The formation of the Gulf Cooperation Council (GCC) in May 1981 in large measure was catalyzed by the perceived Iranian threat to the region. Saudi Arabia, Kuwait, Bahrain, Qatar, the United Arab Emirates (UAE) and Oman formed the organization as an economic, internal security cooperation and defense arrangement. GCC concern for the Iranian threat was reinforced by an abortive coup in December 1981 in Bahrain organized by Iranian-trained and supplied members of the Islamic Front for the Liberation of Bahrain. Reaction by GCC member-states to the coup attempt was a decisive increase in regional diplomatic and economic support for Iraq....

The so-called Steadfastness Front—Syria, Libya, Algeria, the People's Democratic Republic of Yemen (PDRY) and the Palestine Liberation Organization (PLO)—met on May 24, 1982, in Algiers to proclaim that Iran was a friend of the Arabs and to urge that no Arab state help Iraq. While this group officially declared support for Iran, the level of support has varied from Syria's outright condemnation of Iraq to the more nuetral and mediative efforts of the PLO and Algeria.

Arab League foreign ministers (with the exception of Syria and Libya) met in an emergency session in Baghdad in mid-March 1984 and issued a condemnation of Iran's "continuous aggression and its attempts to cross international borders and occupy Iraq's territories." They urged Iran to abide by resolutions calling for an end to hostilities and to accept mediation initiatives to end the conflict.

Despite its isolation resulting from the Egyptian-Israeli peace treaty, Egypt has been considered in some Arab circles as a counterweight to Iran because of its size of population and comparative military strength. Iraqi President Husayn in May 1982 invited Egyptian President Muhammad Mubarek to send troops. Egypt, since 1981, had been contributing arms and ammunition to Iraq. Mubarek declined to dispatch Egyptian forces. But relations between the two countries have drawn closer. Iraqi military missions have visited Cairo in 1982 and 1983. Egyptian Foreign Minister Kamal Hassan Ali stated on March 26, 1984, at the conclusion of a visit to Baghdad that his government fully supported Iraq and would not hesitate to offer any military aid requested. Iraqi President Husayn on May 3 called for Egypt's return to the Arab league. President Mubarek visited Baghdad in March 1985 as a gesture of support for Iraq.

WHAT IS
EDITORIAL OPINION?

This activity may be used as an individualized study guide for students in libraries and resource centers or as a discussion catalyst in small group and classroom discussions.

The capacity to recognize an author's point of view is an essential reading skill. The skill to read with insight and understanding involves the ability to detect different kinds of opinions or bias. Sex bias, race bias, ethnocentric bias, political bias and religious bias are five basic kinds of opinions expressed in editorials and all literature that attempts to persuade. They are briefly defined in the glossary below.

5 Kinds of Editorial Opinion Or Bias

*sex bias— the expression of dislike for and/or feeling of superiority over the opposite sex or a particular sexual minority

*race bias— the expression of dislike for and/or feeling of superiority over a racial group

*ethnocentric bias— the expression of a belief that one's own group, race, religion, culture or nation is superior. Ethnocentric persons judge others by their own standards and values.

*political bias— the expression of political opinions and attitudes about domestic or foreign affairs

*religious bias— the expression of a religious belief or attitude

Guidelines

1. Locate five sentences that provide examples of editorial opinion or bias in any readings from chapter two.

2. Locate five sentences that provide examples of editorial opinion or bias from any of the readings in chapter one.

3. Write down each of the above sentences and determine what kind of bias each sentence represents. Is it *sex bias, race bias, ethnocentric bias, political bias* or *religious bias?*

5. See if you can locate five sentences that are factual statements from the readings in chapter two.

CHAPTER 3

IRANIAN AND IRAQI PERSPECTIVES: IDEAS IN CONFLICT

10 AN IRANIAN PERSPECTIVE

HOW IRAQ STARTED THE WAR

War Information Headquarters of Iran

The following statements were excerpted from a book by the War Information Headquarters of Iran explaining how Iraq was responsible for starting the Iran-Iraq War.

Points to Consider

1. Who is Saddam Hussein and how is he described?
2. What role did the U.S. play in the invasion of Iraq?
3. When and why did Iraq invade Iran?
4. What kind of destruction did U.N. observers describe in Iran?
5. What environmental damage did the Iraqi invasion cause?

War Information Headquarters of Iran, *The Imposed War*, (Tehran, April, 1984) pp. 7-18.

The Iraqi army in its advance inside Iran, left a track of total ruin and desolation behind it.

The painful path of human history is stained with the bloodied footprints of world-conquerors such as Genghiz, Alexander and Hannibal, who wreaked untold havoc on the world, massacred the innocent, and wrecked civilizations.

Since the World Wars of this century, no such ravagers have trampled the earth; except the superpowers who perpetrated carnages of comparable proportions in the lands under their ominous sway. However, the recent years have witnessed the emergence of a petty figure, who seems to have embodied, if not the power, but the lust and savagery of those ancient world-devourers; and one whose crimes,—if not his conquests—are reminiscent of the brutalities of the old conquerors.

These grim lines may sketch the quixotic profile of Saddam Hussein, who once masqueraded as the champion of anti-Zionist campaigns, and who was the chief exponent of ousting Egypt from the Arab community. Yet the forty two months of the Iraqi imposed war have unmasked Saddam's real face, and revealed him as the staunch advocate of conciliation with Egypt, and recognizing Israel.

Islamic Revolution

Following the victory of the Islamic Revolution of Iran, which created a center of social, cultural and political dynamism in the region, the U.S. deputized the Baghdad regime to invade Iran and overthrow its fledgling government, thus attempting to contain the growth of the Islamic Revolution and prevent it from flourishing in the region and disseminating its liberating message to the farthest corners of the globe, inspiring the deprived masses to break the centuries-old yoke of superpowers' dominance.

Ever since the culmination of the Islamic Revolution, the Iraqi regime, mindful of the mission delegated to it, started preparing for an extensive war. It began stockpiling armaments, and cramming its arsenals with the latest

Iraqi Invasion

On 17 September 1980, Iraq abrogated its 1975 treaty with Iran and subsequently attacked the Islamic Republic of Iran in violation of the most sacred principles of international law as well as those of the Charter of the United Nations.

Iranian Government Press Release, April 5, 1985

military hardware which was generously supplied by the superpowers; while at the same time, it was engaged in constructing fully equipped fortifications along its borders with Iran.

Meanwhile, the Iraqi regime, in order to lay the grounds for an outright aggression, started carrying out provoking action on the borders. The series of harassments began right after the victory of the Islamic Revolution. In April 2, 1979, only 50 days after the culmination of the Revolution, Iraqi planes violated the airspace of the border city of Mehran. The following day, a detachment of Iraqi army attacked Qasr-e Shirin; and on April 7, the oil installations of the city were hit by Iraqi rockets.

The Invasion

These aggressive acts of provocation were kept up till September 22, 1980, on which day, the Iraqi army launched its invasion of the Islamic homeland. Up to the outset of the invasion, a total of 636 instances of aggressions comprising air and ground attacks, shelling, looting, cattle-rustling, farm-burning and blasting the oil pipes have been documented and set on record. For instance, the Iraqis carried out an air-strike against Mehran, as well as shelling it by long-range artillery, on May 29, 1980, which claimed the lives of twelve civilians and wounded 36 others. Also on September 3, 1980, Mehran was hit by an Iraqi missile which martyred 2 and injured 5 civilians in that city. Other Iranian border cities, such as Piranshahr, Paveh, Sardasht, Dehloran, Qasr-e Shirin, Naft-Shahr and Musian were also subjected to inhuman Iraqi attacks.

The Iraqi Baath party, having placed at the forefront of its programs the plan for overthrowing the government of the Islamic Republic, in the May 1980, issue of its internal organ titled: "On Our Stance Towards Iran", wrote: "We feel justified to mobilize our best efforts towards overthrowing the racist and Persian regime of Iran, so that a government inclined to friendly ties with Iraq and Arab people, and desirous of good neighborly relations, should take power there."

To this end, Saddam Hussein, launching out into an insane venture called "Qadessiyeh of Saddam", on September 18, 1980, abrogated unilaterally the 1975 border agreement of Algeria, and on September 22, 1980, invaded Iran along a front of 1352 kilometers, penetrating at certain points as deep as 80 kilometers into the Iranian territory. Simultaneously several Iranian cities, including Tehran were bombarded by the Iraqi air force.

Total Ruin

The Iraqi army in its advance inside Iran, left a track of total ruin and desolation behind it, visiting death and disaster on the cities and towns which lay on its sinister path. Cities of Hoveizeh, Qasr-e Shirin, Musian, Sumar and Ozgoleh, were razed to the ground, and numerous villages including some 356 Arab-inhabited villages in Khuzestan province were reduced to ashes and literally wiped out of the map. The Iraqis, moreover, took captive over three thousand civilian Iranian citizens, and Iraqi artillery rained fire and death continuously over the populated areas of the South and Western Iran.

Having occupied vast stretches of the Iranian territory, totalling over 14 thousand square kilometers, the Iraqi rulers put forth haughty demands which betrayed their underlying motive which was overthrowing the government of the Islamic Republic of Iran. . . .

The U.N delegation inspecting the invaded territory in May, 1983, reported that: "The whole area 'Hoveizeh' had been levelled, except for two buildings. There were no trees to be seen. The old bridge across the river Karkh-e-nur had been demolished, and a new bridge had been built."

Saddam's later insistence on destruction of Khorramshahr

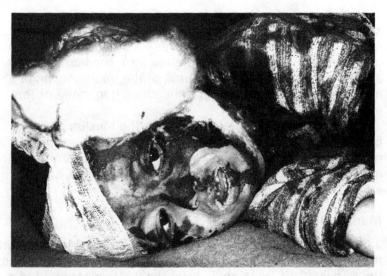
Wounded Child in Hospital

and Qasr-e Shirin revealed that the Baathist regime of Iraq bitterly detested, not only human beings, animals and plants, but anything which could shelter life and living creatures.

When Qasr-e Shirin was liberated, its 12886 housing units and 86 neighboring villages, had been reduced to a wilderness of debris. The U.N. fact-finding team having inspected the devastation declared: "The extent of destruction also gave the impression that other means such as explosive charges and engineering equipment, may have been used."

In the course of the war, the Iraqi troops fearing that some of their cities should be captured by the Iranian forces intact, took to demolishing some of their own cities. Thus in Val-Fajr 4 operation, the Iraqi troops, as though deriving a wicked pleasure from any destruction, even of their own cities, demolished a large portion of the Kurd-inhabited Iraqi city of Panjwin with explosives and engineering equipment. At the time, Iran presented to the world opinion, a documented account of this brutal act of the Iraqi army.

However, during the forty two months of relentless resistance and defense against the aggressors, the combatants of Islam swept back the enemy, liberating all the occupied territories except for one thousand square kilometers which is still held by the enemy. Besides taking back from the Iraqi forces the devastated Iranian cities, the combatants of Islam also penetrated into the Iraqi territory and eliminated the constant threat of the Iraqi long-range artillery which was targeting, from inside Iraq, most of the Iranian border cities.

The Iraqi army, unable to cope with the Muslim combatants in the warfronts, stepped up its attacks on the residential areas and subjecting the cities to missile and aerial attacks, took lives of thousands of civilians, and laid waste thousands of housing units. . . .

Marine Destruction

Besides the destruction which the Iraqi forces inflicted on the cities, they did not spare even the marine environment of the Persian Gulf, causing widespread contamination of this vital waterway by attacking Iranian off-shore oil installations.

During the 230 days of continuous oil-spill from No. 3 Nowruz oil-well, which had been damaged by Iraqi rockets on Jan. 27, 1983, over 460,000 barrels of oil gushed into the Persian Gulf waters, causing serious damage to the marine life, as well as contaminating the coastal areas. The pollution threatened the littoral states with serious shortage of fresh water for supplying which those states depend on desalinating the sea water which was now rendered totally useless for the purpose.

Iran took measures to alleviate the problem by shipping fresh water to the stricken countries, and in the meantime, succeeded, under the most unfavorable circumstances in capping the damaged oil well, on Sept. 18, 1983, solely utilizing the expertise of the workers and technicians of the Iranian Oil Industries. . . .

The Muslim nation of Iran is determined to continue its war against the aggressor, till the fulfilment of its declared conditions, and to decide the outcome of the war which symbolizes the battle of truth against falsity.

May the ultimate triumph crown the devoted efforts of combatants of Islam.

AN IRAQI PERSPECTIVE

HOW IRAN STARTED THE WAR

Iraqi Ministry of Foreign Affairs

*The following statement was excerpted from a position
paper issued by the Iraqi Ministry of Foreign Affairs.*

Points to Consider

1. What are the fundamental ideological differences
    between Iran and Iraq?
2. What provocations toward Iraq occurred after Khomeini's
    rise to power?
3. Why does Iran bear the full responsibility for starting the
    war?
4. How did Iran start the war in 1980?

Iraqi Ministry of Foreign Affairs, *How Iran Started The War,*
October, 1984.

Iran bears the full responsibility for kindling the fires of war as it bears the full responsibility for continuing it all this long time.

One of the first questions Iraqis are asked is, *"Why did you start the war?"*. Disputes between Iraq and Iran have been settled in the past by peaceful talks, not war; most recently in 1975 when Algeria helped to negotiate an agreement on international borders, access to the Shatt al-Arab waterway, and non-interference in each other's internal affairs.

Friction between Iran and Iraq did not actually begin on September 4, 1980. This date marks only the onset of armed hostilities in the Iran-Iraq conflict. The present deterioration of relations between the two countries is directly correlated to Khomeini's rise to power. Khomeini put a new twist on the old disputes over borders, territory, and non-interference, using these sensitive areas to promote discord.

Khomeini's Iran

Fundamental to the current conflict are the basic ideological differences now found between Iran and Iraq. Under Khomeini, Iran has followed a line of religious fanaticism, one which recognizes no political or geographic limits to the expansion of its control and influence. Iraq, on the other hand, adheres to a policy of nationalism, rejecting the domination of religious elements in the administration of the state while espousing freedom of belief and practice and unity among its Peoples. These diametrically opposed ideologies are the core of the Iran-Iraq war.

Almost immediately after coming to power, Khomeini began to focus on the overthrow of the Iraqi government as the first logical stepping-stone in his expansionist policy. A slow, but deliberate, series of provocations ensued, beginning with the new Iranian government's disavowal, in June of 1979, of the 1975 Algiers Accord. Khomeini freed himself from the constraints of this accord under the pretext that it had been concluded by the late shah and sponsored by the United States. The Algiers Accord and its subsequent protocols provided for a definitive settlement of borders and strict adherence to non-interference in internal affairs by joint committees set up for that end. Khomeini disregarded the Algiers Accord, the settlements based upon it and refused to implement them. Khomeini's disregard for this accord put a halt to the committees' work.

Saddam Hussein

While the Iraqi government was extending its goodwill gestures to the new Iranian government and encouraging the development of good relations, Khomeini's representatives were publicly condemning the Iraqi government and claiming the allegiance of Iraqi Muslims, thus sowing division amongst the Moslems of Iraq and between Iraq's Moslems and non-Moslems. As Iran's rhetoric against the Iraqi leadership continued, Iraqi officials proposed to meet with Iranian leaders to discuss bilateral relations. In his address on July 17, 1980, President Saddam Hussein stressed Iraqi support of the Iranian People and expressed the desire for mutual cooperation between the two countries. . . .

Hostile Attitude

Despite Iraq's friendly overtures, the Iranian leadership insisted on its hostile attitude. Throughout March 1980, Iranian officials persisted in their warnings to the Iraqi People to *"Beware of the Ba'ath party and Iraqi leadership."* Khomeini issued a statement in late March urging both the youth and the military of Iraq to rebel against their government and to become heroes in a battle to rid Iraq of the Ba'ath and the extinction of Arab Nationalism.

In an address delivered by his son on March 21, 1980, Khomeini made Iran's position clear: *"We should exert all efforts to export our revolution to other parts of the world. Let us abandon the idea of keeping our revolution within our borders."*

Iran, however, was not leaving its message to chance, *"Iraq is Persian,"* Iran's President stated on April 7, 1980, more than five months before the war began. *"Aden and Baghdad belong to us,"* said Iran's Foreign Minister, Qotob Zada on April 8. Zada went one step further in his remarks the following day, stating that his Government had *"decided to overthrow the Iraqi Government."*

Khomeini reiterated and expanded this theme on a weekly basis throughout April. In an impassioned radio address, Khomeini severely attacked President Hussein and asked the Iraqi army to rebel and topple its government. He accused the Iraqi army of combatting Islam and again declared the urgency of the revolution's march towards Baghdad. In a direct appeal, Khomeini said, *"The Iraqi People should liberate themselves from the claws of the enemy. It should topple this non-Islamic party in Iraq."*

The intransigence of the Iranian position was demonstrated on various occasions. At the beginning of May, 1980, the Iranian President claimed it would not be interference in Iraq's domestic affairs to go to Baghdad to *"liberate"* the Iraqi People because *"We consider the Islamic nation as one and the Imam [Khomeini] is the religious leader for us as well as for Iraq and for all Islamic peoples. [The Imam] feels he is responsible for Iraq as well as Iran."*

Foreign Minister Zada spoke at a press conference in Abu Dhabi where he remained firm in his position on Iraq saying, *"We do not accept any mediation or dialogue with this criminal [Iraqi] regime. . .it must disappear and the People of*

Destabalizing the Region

Khomeini's scheme through the so-called Islamic revolution was to destabilize the region through inciting religious sectarian strife. We in Iraq refuse such a Medieval ideology. Our concept is secular, and we do not mix together affairs of State and religion. Revolutions cannot be imposed from the outside against the free will of the people. We are bound to stand against Khomeini's theories and practices, in defense of our security, well-being and independence.

Iraqi Government Press Release, October 15, 1980.

Iraq want to topple their Government." In a radio address in Tehran a few days later, Zada said that *because the Ba'ath regime practices oppression against the Moslem People of Iraq. . .We shall not come to terms with them."*

Indeed, ever since its assumption of power, the Iranian regime has embarked on a series of provocative acts against the government and People of Iraq. In late 1979, for example, Iran began a series of attacks on diplomatic, consular, cultural, and commercial missions of Iraq. The personnel of the Iraqi Embassy in Tehran, its Consulates in Muhamara (Khorramshahr) and Kermanshah, Iraqi schools in Iran and the Iraqi Airways office in Tehran were all subject to various verbal and physical acts of aggression. . . .

Full Responsibility

Iran bears the full responsibility for kindling the fires of war as it bears the full responsibility for continuing it all this long time.

The regime that has come to power in Iran has arrogated to itself some bizarre privileges which have no basis in international law or in the rules governing relations among peoples: it insists on imposing guardianship not only on Iraq but also on the peoples of the region and indeed on all the world. It has used every available means to interfere in the internal affairs of Iraq and the countries of the region and, indeed, many other countries of the world. It seeks to export its bloodstained and backward system to others, ignoring the fact that that system is a purely internal concern of Iran's and that no one in our world has the right to impose guardianship on others.

In pursuing this anomalous course, the Iranian regime has resorted to all means of committing acts of sabotage and creating chaos and has launched open aggression. Instead of renouncing the expansionist policies and the imperial ambitions of the former regime, it has adopted them as its own. It has upheld the privileges of the former regime, and has used the military power it has inherited from that regime to realize its expansionist aims.

For its part, Iraq has tried with every means at its disposal to reaffirm the necessity of neighborly relations between the two countries and has avoided confrontation with Iran. The Iranian regime, however, has persisted in its aggressive and expansionist policies and continued to fan the fires of dissension, conflict, and war.

From the beginning of 1979 to the start of the armed conflict on 4 September 1980, the Iranian regime committed 249 violations of Iraqi air space, 244 acts of opening fire on, attacking and shelling Iraqi border towns and obstructing navigation in Shatt Al Arab, 3 acts of firing on civil airplanes, 7 acts of shelling of economic facilities, including oil installations. All these acts of aggression are documented in official memoranda which the Iraqi Ministry of Foreign Affairs sent at the time to the Iranian Embassy at Baghdad and the the Iranian Ministry of Foreign Affairs. In a total of 293 official memoranda, we drew the attention of the Iranian side to the gravity of such practices and acts and pointed out that the Iranian authorities bear the responsibility for their effects on the future of neighborly relations between the two countries.

The War Begins

On 4 September 1980 Iran started actual war against Iraq by opening heavy artillery fire on Iraqi border towns, causing losses in lives and severe damage to property and threatening the sovereignty and security of Iraq. In the following days the Iranian armed forces attacked Iraqi oil installations and Iranian military planes launched air raids against the border town of Mendeli. On 12 September, Iranian forces opened fire on an Iraqi ship in Shatt Al Arab and on Iraqi territory in the Basrah area and in Khanaqin. On 17 September, the Iranian authorities announced the closure of Iranian air space to civil aviation and the Hormuz Straits to Iraqi navigation. Iran also announced general mobilization, deployed its armed forces in massive concentrations along the Iraqi border and openly used its regular military forces, including the Iranian air force, in aggression against Iraq. In the period from 18 to 22 September, Iran opened fire 19 times on Iraqi military boats and Iraqi territory in the areas of Basrah, Khaniqin, Qaratu, Mendeli as well as on the Coast guard Command Headquarters at Basrah and the control tower of Iraqi ports along Shatt Al Arab. The Iranian regime also used its air force to attack the oil fields in Naftkhaneh as well as to penetrate Iraqi air space. Between 4 and 22 September, Iranian military leaders issued statements in which they announced their intention to occupy Iraq and its capital, destroy the Iraqi armed forces and erase Iraq from the map of the region.

Iraq was obliged to defend itself against this flagrant aggression and against the blind insistence of the Iranian regime on threatening its security and stability and on interfering in its internal affairs.

Iraq cannot accept guardianship by any one, and it cannot submit to threats and aggression. It had no choice but to fight to defend its sovereignty and dignity and protect the achievements it had realized by the free exercise of its will and by its creative endeavors in the political, economic and cultural fields.

12 AN IRANIAN PERSPECTIVE

IRAQI ATROCITIES

War Information Headquarters of Iran

The following statement was excerpted from a publication by the Iranian War Information Headquarters of the Supreme Defense Council.

Points to Consider

1. How has Iraq violated the Charter of the United Nations and international laws?
2. How often has Iraq used chemical weapons against Iran?
3. What evidence of chemical war by Iraq is cited in the reading?

Iranian War Information Headquarters, *Use Of Chemical Warfare By The Iraqi Forces,* March, 1984.

The latest Iraqi use of chemical weapons against the Iranian forces was so extensive that even the U.S. was compelled to censure the Baghdad regime for it.

Allow me to provide you with a small list of the aggressive acts of the Iraqi regime in the course of the last four years in order to shed more light on the situation: The Iraqi regime has threatened international peace and security and flagrantly and openly violated the aims of the Charter of the United Nations and international laws in numerous cases including the following:

1.   Violation of the Charter of the United Nations by resorting to force for settling disputes and invading the Islamic Republic of Iran with the intention of occupying its territory and overthrowing its regime; failure to seek arbitration as stipulated in the 1975 Algiers Treaty.

2.   Violation of humanitarian principles by destruction of civilian and residential areas in the Islamic Republic of Iran as stated in report S/15834 dated 20th June 1983 issued by the Secretary General's mission to Iran.

3.   Repeated violation of the four Geneva Conventions as stated in report No. S/15834 dated 20th June 1983 of the United Nations' mission sent to Iran and the statements by the International Red Cross regarding the treatment of Iranian P.O.W.s by the Iraqi regime and missile attacks against residential areas.

4.   Violation of all international regulations and conventions regarding the environment and endangering maritime life in the Persian Gulf.

5.   Violation of the 1925 Geneva Protocol regarding the prohibition of the use of chemical weapons as detailed in report No. S/16433 dated 26th March 1984, issued by the United Nations' mission to Iran.

6.   Violation of international laws concerning commercial shipping by attacking commercial vessels in the Persian Gulf for the purpose of causing tension throughout the Persian Gulf region with the consequence of endangering peace, security and the stability of the world economy in view of the vital role of the Persian Gulf region in this respect. . . .

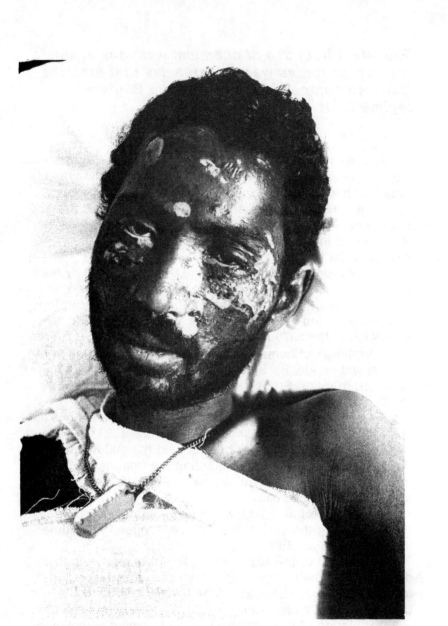

Chemical War Victim

Use of Chemical Warfare by the Iraqi Forces

The Iraqi forces for the fiftieth time throughout the imposed war, on Feb. 27, 1984 employed chemical weapons against the Iranian forces. This latest attack which was launched on a far more massive scale, compared to previous ones, disabled over 1,100 combatants of Islam in Hur al-Hoveizeh operational theatre.

One of the victims of the attack, Ali-Akbar Fameely, from the Basij popular forces, speaking to a group of foreign journalists in Labbafi-Nejad hospital, Tehran, described the Iraqi attack thus:

"It was Monday morning Feb. 27, 1984 when shortly after we heard some Iraqi planes flying overhead, we noticed some black stuff which has settled on our equipment. All of a sudden we found our weapons and whatever else was out in the open, covered with a thin dark layer; and this happened in a very extensive area.

"our nostrils started burning and itching, which was followed with breathlessness and suffocation. Within six hours from the exposure of such other symptoms like blurred, irritated eyes, and a painful sensation on sensitive parts of the body appeared on most of us."

Thirty percent of those affected, who were suffering from a wide spectrum of symptoms, were transferred to hospitals in Tehran. The injuries ranged from nausea and dizziness to severe skin lesions and enormous blisters; from partial or total lack of vision to sore throat and asphyxiation.

A Global Disgrace

The Austrian doctors treating ten injured combatants, have identified the cause of the injuries as chemical gases of various descriptions.

Doctor Ernest Wolner, head of the second surgical clinic of the public hospital says:

"Eight of the patients are suffering from superficial acid burns of the skin. Two others are under intensive care with lesions of inner organs as well, including a drop in white blood corpuscles."[1]

1. Nicosia, AP. March 5, '84

The Chemically Wounded

Since the beginning of the Kheibar operation up to the present more than 200 chemically wounded soldiers have been admitted in Labbafi-Nejad Medical Centre, with wide-ranging variety of ailments and damages.

Iranian Government Press Release, February 1984.

In a radio interview Dr. Herbert Mandel, head of the CCU ward of Akaha hospital in Vienna announced that *"According to analyses conducted in the toxicological laboratory of the city of Ghent, Belgium, the Iranian soldiers had been exposed to a toxic chemical called mycotoxin, differently known as yellow-rain or mustard gas. The subsequent tests have corroborated this prognosis."*[2]

The use of noxious gases has also been confirmed by the medical committee of the international Red Cross Organization which visited the victims in Tehran hospitals. In its statement the Red Cross Committee declared: *"The nature of injuries and symptoms examined on those visited in Tehran hospitals indicate that the said injuries have been caused by certain compounds the production of which has been banned by international laws."*

Says Herbert Benzer, head of intensive care ward of the second surgical clinic of Vienna:

"The symptoms the patients show are very similar to those registered in soldiers during World War I when mustard gas was used.". . .[3]

The latest Iraqi use of chemical weapons against the Iranian forces was so extensive that even the U.S. was compelled to censure the Baghdad regime for it. In its March 9, '84 issue, the American daily, New York Times, quoting informed sources, wrote: *"There is sufficient evidence available to the Reagan Administration to prove the recent charges brought against Iraq that she had used chemical weapons against Iran."*

2. Vienna, AP. March 10, '84
3. Vienna, Reuter March 6, '84

Britain which was herself accused of selling chemical weapons to Iraq, nonetheless declared that she would closely investigate Iraq's use of chemical weapons.

French cabinet spokesman Max Gallo, condemning use of chemical weapons, called for signing an international agreement, banning the use of chemical warfare.[4]

Sir Geoffrey Howe, the foreign secretary of Britain expressed support of his government of delegating a fact finding committee to investigate the matter, while there is sufficient evidence to prove complicity of England in supplying Iraq with chemical hardware. One such evidence was discovery of toxic chemicals in an Iraqi ship docked in the port of Normandy, which ship had loaded at Liverpool and was bound for Iraq via Kuwait.

In this connection, the Labor Party representative in the Parliament, Tony Bankes, speaking to a group of reporters, described the British government's providing of chemical weapons to Iraq as "a disgraceful transaction."[5]

The American daily, Washington Post, in its March 8, '84 issue, in connection with Iraq's use of chemical warfare wrote: *"The western reporters who were taken to the battle fields in which the Iranian and Iraqi forces had clashed, noticed that the bodies of the Iranians left in the scene did not bear any trace of bullet or other type of wounds, but that they had apparently died of bleeding from their ears and noses. . .Some unknown substance might have knocked them unconscious and caused the internal bleeding. And a diplomat was wondering why there were no such symptoms as blisters, which are commonly associated with mustard gas, evident on the bodies of the Iranians. . .The mustard gas being noxious, irritates skin, lungs and the eyes, while, this other is in liquid form, causing severe wounds, and if it comes in contact with any portion of the skin, totally destroys that part."*

---

4. Pugwash Conference in its meeting in Geneva, on Feb. 14, 1984, declaring that some 13 countries, including Iraq, had used chemical weapons, also said that the French government had provided Iraq with chemical weapons.

5. London, Reuter.

The enormity of crimes committed by the Iraqi regime this time reached an extent at which even Javier Perez de Cuellar, the U.N. Secretary General no longer capable of ignoring it, had to severely condemn the use of chemical weapons....

A Futile Attempt to Escape a Great Disgrace

In spite of all these incontrovertible evidences which leave no doubt as to Iraq's use of chemical warfare, the Iraqi rulers in a vain bid to cover up their crimes, denied using any chemical weapons. Whereas, besides purchasing chemical hardware from foreign countries, Iraq possesses, as it has been stated by her military and diplomatic sources, three chemical weapon manufacturing plants.

The criminal acts of the Baghdad regime were so flagrant that this time, Iraq's denial was not taken seriously even by those media which have usually come out in full support of that regime.

Flagrant Flouting of Internationally Respected Rules.

The Iraqi regime uses chemical warfare in the face of the fact that she is one of 120 signatories of the Geneva Protocol which outlaws chemical, biological, and other types of noxious and asphyxiating weapons. The 1925 Geneva Protocol which was later re-affirmed by the United Nations Statement B (21) 2162 expressly banned employment of the chemical weapons. . . .

Undoubtedly keeping silent in the face of these criminal acts by the Iraqi regime would amount to an encouraging gesture towards a would-be aggressor to perpetrate a similar crime in some other spot in the world.

"The Iraqi regime's use of chemical warfare stands as an unsettling reminder that the world is susceptible of plunging into an arms race in relation with chemical weapons which inflicted over one million casualties in the two World Wars."

AN IRAQI PERSPECTIVE

IRANIAN ATROCITIES

Riyadh M.S. Al-Qaysi

*Riyadh M.S. Al-Qaysi made the following statement in his
capacity as the permanent representative of Iraq to the
United Nations.*

Points to Consider

1. What request was made to Iraq by the United Nations
   Secretary General?
2. How did Iraq respond to this letter?
3. How was Iran using its border towns and villages?
4. What proposal does Iraq suggest to protect civilian
   populations from the war?

Excerpted from a letter dated 10 March 1985 from the permanent
representative of Iraq to the United Nations addressed to the
Secretary General.

The Iranian regime proceeded to commit new crimes against Iraqi civilians and to cause increased bloodshed.

We have received your letter dated 9 March 1985 addressed to the President of the Republic and, in accordance with His Excellency's directives, I should like to set forth the view of my Government with respect to its contents.

When, on 9 June 1984, you called upon Iran and Iraq to halt deliberate attacks on purely civilian areas, Iraq immediately agreed to your appeal in the letter addressed to you by the President of the Republic on 10 June 1984.

In the letter of the President of the Republic, just as in the two letters addressed to you by myself on 21 and 27 June 1984, we stressed that a halt to attacks on towns and villages involved the need to ascertain that Iranian border towns and villages were not used as centres for the massing of Iranian forces. Unfortunately, however, this practical and sensible request was ignored. When you appointed the mission to investigate incidents in violation of the agreement, we requested the United Nations Secretariat to place observers in all sectors of operations so that observation might be effective and immediate. The Iranian side, however, at first refused to host the mission inside Iran and then agreed to its being stationed in Teheran only, thereby, prompting you to retain the mission in Baghdad only.

Iranian Border Towns

It was clear to us that the insistence of the rulers of Iran on keeping the mission away from the sectors of belligerent operations had the aim of preventing United Nations observation of the use of Iranian border towns and villages as concentration centres and of allowing them to violate the agreement whenever they wished to do so for political or military motives in accordance with their whims and objectives and with the antagonisms and conflicts going on among them.

In fact, our reconnaissance had ascertained that the Iranian towns I mentioned in my letter to you of 27 June 1984 were used as centres for massing forces. We annexed

By Bill Sanders
© by and permission of *News America Syndicate*

to that letter a list containing the names of the Iranian units being massed in the towns of Abadan, Mohammarah, Khrosrowabad, Ahvaz, Hoveyzeh, Bisitin and Andimeshk. Since that time, a number of military attacks have been launched against the Iraqi borders, namely on 20 October 1984, and on 1 February and 2-3 March 1985. Over the past months there have also been numerous violations of the agreement caused by the inadequacy of the supervision procedures and the arbitrary Iranian interpretations of the agreement.

Moreover, the Iranian authorities have not, in recent times, ceased from giving vent to sudden and repeated threats to bombard our cities using as pretexts incidents taking place during military operations to which the terms of the agreement do not apply. In this connection, I single out for special mention the threats made by the President of the Iranian Republic on 8 February 1985.

Civilian Casualties

This month, while the Security Council was discussing a very sensitive and important issue relating to the war, namely the suffering of tens of thousands of prisoners, in an attempt on the part of the United Nations to find a solution to their plight, the Iranian regime issued, for no good reason, a warning to the effect that it would shell the city of Basra. It then gave effect to its warning by deliberately shelling the city of Basra on 5 March 1985, causing the death and wounding of a number of civilian inhabitants and the destruction of their homes and personal property. As I explained to you in my letter of 6 March 1985, the pretexts used by the Iranian regime for committing this crime are baseless. The Iraqi bombardment that took place on 4 March 1985 was aimed at a factory in the outskirts of the city of Ahvaz, a target which is not covered by the agreement of 12 June 1984. The Iranian regime, instead of having recourse to the procedures agreed upon with you with respect to the investigation of such incidents by requesting the United Nations mission to visit the site of the bombardment, issued its above-mentioned warning and deliberately shelled the city of Basra. In accordance with those procedures, and before reacting to that deliberate crime, we requested the United Nations mission stationed in Baghdad to go to the city of Basra to investigate the bombardment. The Iranian regime, however, once again violated the rules of those procedures and did not agree to accord your mission safe conduct so that it might carry out its task.

It was clear to concerned observers that the deliberate bombardment of Basra on 5 March 1985 had the objective of distracting attention from the deliberations of the Security Council with respect to the prisoners of war, and even of sabotaging the Council's efforts to find a humane and effective solution to their suffering. Accordingly, instead of making a positive contribution to the solution of this human tragedy, the Iranian regime proceeded to commit new crimes against Iraqi civilians and to cause increased bloodshed.

I should like to stress to you, Mr. Secretary-General, that it was Iraq that was the author of the idea of concluding a special agreement to prevent attacks on towns and villages. The President of the Republic of Iraq made a declaration to

Prisoners of War

Let us consider for a little while the tragedy of the prisoners of war. The Tehran authorities have always treated Iraqi POWs from the political premise of Iranian expansionist territorial ambitions in Iraq. Not only have they killed, in a premeditated manner, those POWs who refused to succumb to their will, but also planted amongst the rest of them Iranian elements who had resided previously in Iraq. The aim of this measure is to spread psychological terror and impose political and physical oppression with a view to undermining the POW's allegiance to their country.

Iraq Ministry of Foreign Affairs, September 27, 1985.

that effect in June of 1984. The idea was also embodied in Security Council resolution 540 (1983), which was accepted by Iraq and rejected by Iran. Iraq had, in all sincerity, adhered to the agreement of 12 June 1984. It has co-operated with you and with the Security Council in order to find an overall solution to the conflict and, in like manner, in order to find solutions to the pressing humanitarian problems arising out of the conflict, whereas the Iranian regime has manifested not the slightest degree of co-operation and has continued to direct accusations against the Council and the United Nations and to handle sensitive humanitarian issues on the basis of opportunistic political motives and in accordance with the cheap settling of accounts that it deems appropriate.

Protecting Civilians

Accordingly, in spite of our assured desire to comply with your appeal and spare civilians the afflictions of war, and in spite of our fervent solicitude that the situation should not escalate, we cannot leave matters ambivalent and fluid so that violations might recur. . . .

We believe that the practical solution to this question, and to all the questions of a humanitarian character arising out of the conflict, would come about through the establishment of direct contacts by yourself with authorized representatives of the two parties to draw up clear and agreed principles, rules and guarantees for an agreement to prevent the deliberate bombardment of purely civilian population centres and for establishing a modality for tackling other matters. Thus, we would be fully able to ensure the safety of the population of our country so as not to leave them exposed to the whims of the rulers of Teheran, who threaten their lives and security whenever they wish, and we would also ensure proper handling of other humanitarian issues. I should like to express my readiness to travel immediately to New York to hold direct contacts with you for that purpose. We would also welcome your visiting Iraq should you wish to do so.

14 AN IRANIAN PERSPECTIVE

ENDING THE WAR

Iranian Ministry of Foreign Affairs

*The following statements were excerpted from THE
IMPOSED WAR, a book by the Iranian Ministry of Foreign
Affairs and a United Nations speech by Rajaie Khorassani,
the Iranian Ambassador to the United Nations.*

Points to Consider

1. What does Iran mean by a lasting peace?
2. How are the civil and criminal liabilities of Iraq defined?
3. What is meant by the term reparations?
4. Under what political conditions would Iran stop military
   action?

Ministry of Foreign Affairs, *The Imposed War* (Iran, 1985), pp. 140-52
and a United Nations speech by Rajaie Khorassani, October 20,
1982.

The fascist and racist Ba'athist party of Iraq, lacks the necessary competence to rule over Iraq, and be the representative of the people of Iraq.

A Model U.N. Resolution

The government of the Islamic Republic of Iran has repeatedly stated its desire for establishing a just and lasting peace in the Persian Gulf region. This does not mean that anything labeled as peace will be acceptable for Iran. A lasting peace is different from one that would only be used by the adventurist government of Iraq for reorganization and rearmament for the next round. . . .

A resolution, to be fair and just, must reflect the realities that have existed on the scene between Iran and Iraq. The model resolution that the Islamic Republic of Iran would propose, would read as follows:

The General Assembly

Having considered the item entitled "the consequences of the prolongation of the armed conflict between Iran and Iraq".
Reaffirming the inadmissibility of the use of threat of force in international relations.
Recalling the obligation of states under the Geneva Convention relative to the Protection of Civilian Persons in Time of War, of 12 August 1949.
Recalling the commitment of states to provide by the provisions of the Charter, and specifically Articles 33 and 37, in resolving their disputes.
Reiterating the right of all states to self defense as recognized in Article 51 of the Charter.
1. Condemns Iraq for having initiated armed aggression in its dispute with Iran before the exhaustion of all peaceful means available within the framework of the Charter.
2. Deplores the occupation of Iranian territory by Iraq and the attempt of Iraq to use that illegal occupation to extract political concessions.

90

3. Also condemns Iraq for having concentrated her war efforts, for almost two years, primarily on civilian life in Iran, resulting in abhoring crimes against humanity in violation of the Geneva Convention relative to the Protection or Civilian Persons in Time of War, of 12 August 1949.

4. Reaffirms the right of the people of Iran to receive reparations for the losses in life and property inflicted upon them by Iraq's aggression, and the duty of Iraq to assist in restoring all civilian installations that she deliberately destroyed in the territorities under her illegal occupation.

5. Calls upon Iran and Iraq to end all military operations to resolve their disputes by peaceful means, in accordance with the provisions of the Charter.

6. Welcomes the efforts of the Secretary General to mediate between the two countries and invites him to continue his efforts of mediation. . . .

Liabilities of Iraq

The facts establish the criminality of the Iraqi regime and the criminal and aggressive position of the rulers of Iraq. Besides, the legal and defensive stand adopted by the Islamic Republic of Iran in this regard was explained.

Now, we shall briefly look into the international liability of the Ba'athist regime of Iraq as regards the aggressive and expansionist policy of that regime.

The Legal Consequences of the Liabilities of the Iraqi Regime:

The liability of the Iraqi regime for the imposition of war on the Islamic Republic of Iran are both civil and criminal.

A. Civil Liabilities of the Iraqi regime:

"Injury" is universally regarded as a violation of another's right for which the injured must be compensated. The principle is respected by national as well as international laws, in violation of which right, the injured party should be redressed in a manner as to be freed in as much as possible, from the effects of the offense, so that the status existing before the commission of offense is restored. . . .

Therefore, obviously enough the Ba'athist regime of Iraq is bound to pay reparations for the material and spiritual damages and human losses caused by the aggressive war it imposed on Iran; this responsibility emanates from the violation of the internationally accepted principle of "Jus Ad Bellum". In other words a war of aggression creates liability on the part of the aggressor government. It is on this very principle that Article 231 of the Treaty of Versailles considers the Government of Germany and other forces of axis as responsible for the payment of reparations for all the damages inflicted on allied forces as the result of a war of aggression imposed by Germany on such countries. Article 19 of the draft law of the Commission on International Law, on the responsibility of states, deems the war of aggression as an international crime, on the basis of which the said Commission codified the international law. . . .

The damages, as a whole, inflicted by the war imposed upon Iran by Iraq and liability for payment of reparations lie with the aggressive ruling regime of Iraq. . . .

B. The Criminal Responsibility of the Iraqi Political Leaders and Commanders and Personnel of the Iraqi Armed Forces:

The fascist and racist Ba'athist party of Iraq, which has excelled all criminals of the human history, even the once Nazis of Germany, has violated all principles and laws governing international relations, lacks the necessary competence to rule over Iraq, and be the representative of the people of Iraq. Therefore, if the Government of the Islamic Republic of Iran, which is still exposed to Iraqi aggressions after two years since the beginning of the aggression of the Ba'athist regime of Iraq is still suffering from irreparable financial and human losses, wants the international community to punish the aggressor, it is because of this fact that this regime, similar to other criminals, who commit acts against the peace and security of the international community, lacks, from the viewpoint of the international law, the necessary good will to continue its rule. As a historical example, we may cite Nazism and the crimes they (the Nazis) committed against the humanity and the world reaction to it.

After the defeat of the Nazi Germany, the governments

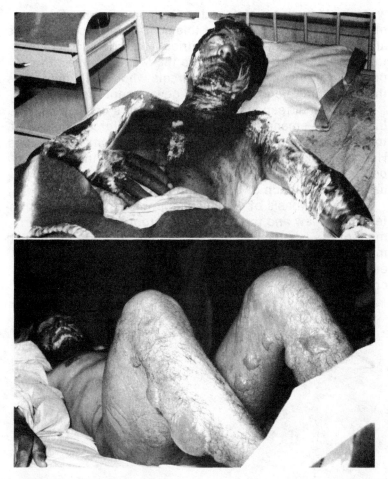

Chemical War Victims

that had suffered from the crimes and aggressive acts of Hitler and had been damaged, in addition to arresting and trying the leaders of the Nazi Party and the perpetrators of the crimes committed by Nazis, made the Nazis pay war reparations for the damages they had inflicted upon others whereby they also disintegrated Germany. But the Government of Iran, as the victim of this aggression, does not have any ambition to the other countries' territories and believes that the Iraqi territory belongs to the Muslim and brotherly people of Iraq and that it is the Iraqis who should determine their own future and the form of government they prefer.

The criminal responsibility of the leaders of the present Iraqi regime emanates from their resort to force. This resort to force has been in violation of all international regulations. Hence, in accordance with these regulations, the perpetrators, and thereby the ruling regime in Iraq becomes liable for its breach of these regulations. . . .

It is on the basis of undeniable principles of the public international law and the accepted customs, that the Government of the Islamic Republic of Iran insists upon the punishment of the aggressor as a principal condition for the establishment of a just and lasting peace between the two countries.

ENDING THE WAR

Iraqi Ministry of Foreign Affairs

The following statements were excerpted from a speech by Tariq Aziz before the United Nations Security Council. Tariq Aziz is deputy Prime Minister and Minister of Foreign Affairs of the Republic of Iraq.

Points to Consider

1. What two kinds of settlements to end the war has the United Nations pursued?
2. What did U.N. Resolution 540 attempt to do?
3. How has Iraq cooperated with attempts to end the war?
4. How has Iran obstructed efforts to end the war?

Excerpted from a speech by Iraqi Foreign Minister Tariq Aziz before the U.N. Security Council, February 18, 1986.

We pointed out that the Iranian regime was not interested in reaching any arrangements that would spare the Arab Gulf region the dangers of war.

From the beginning of Iran's aggression on Iraq on 4 September 1980 to the end of 1982, the Council and the General Assembly were concerned, first and foremost, with bringing the war to an end and achieving a comprehensive settlement to the conflict. I refer here in particular to the Council's important resolution 514, adopted on 12 July, 1982, and to resolution 37/3 adopted by the General Assembly on 22 October, 1982. However, the years 1983, 1984 and 1985 regrettably witnessed a new tendency in the UN Secretariat and the Security Council which gave greater attention to secondary matters arising from the conflict and reduced the emphasis on the comprehensive settlement which the Council had previously stressed.

U.N. Resolution 540

These attempts began in 1983, when the Gulf region faced the effects of the continuation of the war. The Council adopted on 31 October, 1983, resolution 540, which was the first resolution not to deal with all the elements of the conflict comprehensively, but concentrated instead upon some specific elements. The Resolution called for the immediate cessation of all hostilities in the Gulf region, including all sea-lanes, navigable waterways, harbor works, terminals, offshore installations and all ports with direct or indirect access to the sea. Although the said resolution offered no comprehensive solution to the conflict and was limited only to one theater of military operations, and although its implementation from the practical point of view would lead to the prolongation of the war on land and to the minimization of international concern over the dispute and hence the reduction of pressure for a comprehensive settlement, Iraq at the time accepted the resolution. This position on the part of Iraq was in harmony with its firm stand from the inception of the conflict to cooperate with the Security Council and the Secretariat in all means leading to a comprehensive peace. Iraq also accepted the resolution out of its sense of responsibility towards security and stability in the Gulf region and towards those that have trade links with the region.

The Iranian Regime

On its part, the Iranian regime, which was complaining noisily about what was described at the time as "the oil slick", and the dangers of environmental pollution, rejected that resolution, which would have solved that and other issues, amongst which were the safety of trade, oil exports, and sparing civilian population centers the dangers of war. The Iranian regime also rejected, without an official declaration, even the efforts exerted then by some States to ensure a de facto implementation of the said resolution. We explained then to the Organization and to all the States that approached us the reasons behind Iran's rejection of the resolution. We pointed out that the Iranian regime which had been planning an offensive for the occupation of the Basrah area, was not interested in reaching any arrangements that would spare the Arab Gulf region the dangers of war. Indeed the Iranian regime considered the arrangements contained in Resolution 540 an impediment to its preparations for invasion. While preparing for the offensive, the sole concern of the regime was to occupy the international public opinion and the Organization, through lies in order to win time. In fact, the Iranian offensive against the area of Basrah took place in February of 1984, and turned out to be a large-scale attack with the clear military objective of occupying the southern part of Iraq . . . .

Iranian Actions

On 7 June, 1983, the President of the Republic of Iraq proposed the conclusion of a special agreement between Iraq and Iran under the auspices of the United Nations to abstain from attacking population centers. That proposal was rejected by Iran. Resolution 540 (1983) of your Council contained a specific paragraph calling for the immediate cessation of all military operations against civilian targets including cities and residential areas. But Iran rejected that resolution also, as it is well known.

Before it carried out its major offensive to occupy the southern part of Iraq in February 1984, Iran had not been interested in reaching any agreement on this issue, as it was only content with its misleading propaganda campaigns against Iraq in this respect. But after we destroyed that major offensive which left Iran in need of a breathing space to prepare for yet another, it began to show interest in this matter and call upon the Organization to take action on it. The Secretary General appealed to both parties, on 9 June, 1984, to halt all deliberate attacks against purely civilian population centers. Unlike the manner with which it has dealt with the resolutions and initiatives of the Organization, Iran accepted the said appeal immediately. Iraq, of course, also accepted the appeal, for it agreed with its usual stand and with the proposal announced by the President of the Republic of Iraq a year earlier. As a result, the agreement of 12 June, 1984 came into being on the abstention from deliberate military attacks against purely civilian population centers.

Implementing the Agreement

In order to ensure the faithful implementation of that agreement and to prevent it from being exploited to prepare for aggression, I addressed two letters to the UN Secretary General in which I warned against the utilization of Iranian border towns and villages for the purposes of military concentrations in preparation for a new Iranian offensive against Iraq; an offensive the launching of which the Iranian officials, continued to threaten. I mentioned, in my letter of 27 June, 1984 to the Secretary General the names of the Iranian towns and villages in which Iranian forces were concentrated together with the names of the military units placed therein. I also requested the UN Secretariat to provide a sufficient number of observers in all the sectors of operations, so that their inspection would be immediate and accurate on a battle front extending over 1180 kilometers along which on both sides were tens of towns and villages.

This proposal, however, was not considered and the Iranian regime refused in the beginning even to receive the team appointed by the Secretary General to inspect the implementation of the agreement inside Iran, demanding that the team should remain outside Iran. Afterwards, it agreed, under considerable pressure, to let the team stay only in Tehran refusing its presence in, or periodic inspection visits to, other Iranian towns and villages. . . .

A Comprehensive Settlement

In spite of the anguish and the human and material losses caused by the two major Iranian offensives in 1984 and 1985, the attention of the Security Council and the world organization was focused in the first place on secondary questions arising from the conflict, while no concentrated effort was exerted towards a comprehensive settlement. We warned strongly against this approach, and said that it would not in fact serve the objective of a comprehensive peace but would serve the Iranian plan of deception to continue war and aggression against Iraq with the aim of occupying its lands, imposing full hegemony on the Arab Gulf Area, enslaving its peoples, plundering its wealth and spreading anarchy and destruction therein. . . .

The Security Council is faced in the conflict before you with a strange and grave situation whereby one of the parties to the conflict insists on violating all the fundamental rules of international law.

On top of this stand as regards international law, the Iranian regime adopts a strange position in dealing with the Security Council. The Iranian regime refuses to participate in the deliberations of the Council on the conflict and imposes on the Council conditions unprecedented in the history of the United Nations or international practices.

EXAMINING COUNTERPOINTS

This activity may be used as an individualized study guide for students in libraries and resource centers or as a discussion catalyst in small group and classroom discussions.

The Point

On September 22, 1980 Iraq invaded Iran along a front of 1352 kilometers, penetrating at certain points as deep as 80 kilometers into the Iranian territory. Simultaneously several Iranian cities, including Tehran were bombarded by the Iraqi air force.

The Iraqi army in its advance inside Iran, left a track of total ruin and desolation behind it, visiting death and disaster on the cities and towns which lay on its sinister path.

The Counterpoint:

Iran bears the full responsibility for kindling the fires of war as it bears the full responsibility for continuing it all this long time.

The regime that has come to power in Iran has arrogated to itself some bizarre privileges which have no basis in international law or in the rules governing relations among peoples: it insists on imposing guardianship not only on Iraq but also on the peoples of the region and indeed on all the world. It has used every available means to interfere in the internal affairs of Iraq and the countries of the region and, indeed, many other countries of the world.

Guidelines

Social issues are usually complex, but often problems become oversimplified in political debates and discussion. Usually a polarized version of social conflict does not adequately represent the diversity of views that surround social conflicts.

Examine the counterpoints above. Then write down other possible interpretations of this issue than the two arguments stated in the counterpoints above.

CHAPTER 4

THE GULF WAR AND U.S. POLICY

16

OVERVIEW: U.S. POLICY OPTIONS

From the beginning of the conflict, there has been considerable debate over U.S. policy toward Iran and Iraq. Some observers have contended that the U.S. course of neutrality has rendered U.S. policy on the war impotent. They reportedly called for options that would "tilt" the United States toward Iraq. Others have perceived that, if Iraq should carry out its threats to Iran's oil export capabilities, Iran will likely respond with actions that could widen the conflict. Thus, it is essential, in this view, that regional countries and other interested parties make a concerted effort to bring pressure on the two belligerents to exercise restraint. Should there be an escalation of the war, the entire Gulf could become embroiled with obvious regional and worldwide implications, including spillover effects on the Arab-Israeli conflict, the Western economies, and the potential for superpower confrontation.

Those favoring a "tilt" in U.S. policy toward Iraq consider that the short-term interests of the United States and its allies would be served by helping preserve Iraq's sovereignty and preventing the installation of a Shi'ite revolutionary government in Baghdad. The United States can assist in the prevention of an Iraqi economic collapse through the export of U.S. technological expertise and services, and by loans

Richard M. Preece, *The Iran-Iraq War,* Foreign Affairs Division, Library of Congress, March, 1986.

and guarantees, including the Export-Import Bank. They argue that Iraq strategically is important to these interests in that it protects the vulnerable Gulf oil-producing states from Iranian military power and restrains Iranian subversive ambitions. Should Iraq collapse, wider U.S. interests in the Middle East would be threatened.

The advocates of a "tilt" toward Iraq point to the prevailing trend that, over the long term, a war of attrition favors Iran and that Ayatollah Khomeini will never negotiate a settlement until Iraq collapses. They contend that the United States needs Iraq for leverage against Syria; if Iraq collapses, and a Syrian-Iranian axis is formed, Syria will achieve new regional predominance, thereby increasing Soviet influence. Iraq, since 1975, has distanced itself from its formerly close relations with the Soviet Union; despite recent increases in Soviet military supplies, Baghdad maintains its independence from possible Soviet leverage. With respect to U.S. policy goals in the Middle East, Iraq has indicated its acceptance of Israel's right to exist and Baghdad did support U.S. policy in Lebanon in 1983. It has ceased to support international terrorism, having expelled the Abu Nidal faction. Baghdad also has invited Amnesty International for discussions over human rights issues in Iraq. Iran, on the other hand, is lending support to terrorism through training, financing and equipping various groups, and Tehran is suspected for its complicity in the bombings in Lebanon and Kuwait and other incidents of terrorism. The Khomeini regime's human rights record is atrocious. The greatest danger facing Iraq is economic strangulation and, so long as Khomeini remains in power, the war of attrition is likely to be unrelenting. The United States and its allies should at all costs prevent Iranian success. Restoration of diplomatic ties with Baghdad in November 1984 would seem to underscore this determination.

Those critical of an Iraqi option reportedly contend that such a "tilt" toward Iraq serves no useful purpose. They consider that Iran, in the longer-term, is of greater strategic importance to U.S. interests and outweighs other short-term considerations. While there are few expectations for any improvement in U.S.-Iranian relations so long as the current Tehran regime retains power, a "tilt" toward Iraq tends to discourage longer-term moderation in, and future ties with,

Iran. Iran remains the strategic buffer between the Soviet Union and the Gulf; closer U.S. relations with Iraq would tend to draw Iran nearer to the Soviet Union and weaken the nonaligned and anti-Soviet position held by many in the Tehran regime. In this sense, the renewal of U.S.-Iraqi relations serves no useful purpose. From the fall of 1983, with the influx of large deliveries of Soviet weapons to Iraq, Iraqi-Soviet relations have dramatically drawn closer. Some critics argue that Iraq is endeavoring to provoke Iran in making good its threat of closing the Gulf in order to draw in U.S. and other forces into the Gulf conflict, thereby inflicting losses on Iran that Iraq is incapable of accomplishing by itself. In any event, Iran has limited capabilities to close the Gulf.

Others contend that there is no apparent visible role for the United States to play in the conflict; with limited leverage on either side, the United States should remain on the sidelines. Direct U.S. aid to Iraq would only give Iran more reason to prolong the war. The costs of potential U.S. involvement would be high. In any case, the current military stalemate, which drains the energies and resources of both the Tehran and Baghdad regimes, serves U.S. interests and prevents either of them from threatening the Gulf Arab states through military aggression or subversion. The Husayn regime in Baghdad is no better than the Khomeini regime in Teheran. U.S. involvement could jeopardize delicate mediation efforts designed to bring the two belligerents to the bargaining table, and could lead to escalation of the war . . . .

Soviet Interests and Involvement in Iran and Iraq

A leading U.S. policy concern is that the Iran-Iraq conflict will open opportunities for Soviet exploitation, thereby enabling Moscow to enhance its position vis-a-vis the United States in the Gulf region. The nature of the Soviet threat, however, is subject to wide-ranging debate and, since the change of leadership in Moscow, new patterns of Soviet policy may emerge. While Moscow has tended to avoid large risks in the Middle East during the recent past, nevertheless it continues to perceive that it has important and legitimate interests in the region.

For the Soviet Union, the Persian Gulf lies proximate to its southern border and Moscow, as it seeks to increase its influence among regional countries, cannot remain indifferent to political and military developments in the region. Former Soviet Chairman Leonid Brezhnev acknowledged that the Gulf was an area of vital Western interests on Dec. 10, 1980, in New Delhi when he proposed a multilateral agreement for the demilitarization and neutralization of the Gulf region. Nevertheless, the Soviet Union has opposed all U.S. efforts to defend those interests through the establishment of a military presence in the Gulf/Indian Ocean region.

Moscow faces constraints to any policy initiative aimed at exploiting opportunities arising from the Iran-Iraq war. Because of Iran's size, location, population, and common border with the U.S.S.R., the Soviets perceive Iran as strategically more important than Iraq. Since the Iranian revolution, Moscow has aimed at normalizing and improving its political and economic relations with Tehran. But it has avoided any overwhelming commitment toward supporting Iran lest its ties with Iraq and its standing in other parts of the Arab world be eroded. Soviet neutrality in the conflict, in consequence, has been translated into maintaining a controlled supply of arms to both sides.

Soviet relations with Iraq had been good until the mid-1970's when they began to sour, despite a 1972 Treaty of Friendship and Cooperation. Iraq subsequently started to diversify its sources of arms and imported Western — including American — technology and equipment. During the first two years of the Iran-Iraq conflict, Moscow was cool to Iraqi requests for additional supplies of military equipment and spare parts. Iraq responded by executing or exiling members of the Iraqi Communist Party, and was openly critical of Soviet interference and actions in the Middle East, particularly its invasion of Afghanistan. At the same time, increased trade and other ties between Iran and the Soviet Union were largely induced by Iranian dependence on Soviet transit routes following the Iraqi capture of Iran's largest port at Khorramshahr. Iran's considerable economic difficulties led to barter arrangements with East European countries and to an influx of large numbers of Soviet and Eastern bloc exports and advisers.

Despite the intense anti-Americanism of the Iranian regime, Soviet influence does not predominate in Tehran. In fact, the Iranian regime presently continues to identify the Soviet Union as another manifestation of the "satanic forces" with which its revolution is struggling in eternal conflict. Iran's mistrust of the Soviet Union is bolstered by historical experience and by the Tehran regime's policy of nonalignment. In addition, Iran opposes the Soviet presence in Afghanistan and aids the resistance forces. . . .

Evolution of U.S. Policy toward the Iran-Iraq Conflict

Until the reestablishment of diplomatic relations with Baghdad on Nov. 26, 1984, official U.S. relations with Iran and Iraq had been limited. Iraq had severed diplomatic relations with the United States during the 1967 Arab-Israeli war, but both countries had maintained interest sections in each other's capitals. It is unlikely that renewed official ties will increase U.S. leverage over Baghdad. The United States broke relations with Iran in April 1980 following the seizure of the American Embassy and its occupants in Tehran the previous November. Iran's intense anti-Americanism — a central factor in that country's internal political dynamics since its revolution in 1979 — precludes the likelihood of a reestablishment of U.S. Iranian ties so long as the Islamic Republican Party (IRP) under Ayatollah Khomeini retains power.

Since mid-1983, U.S. official contacts with Baghdad have increased and have led credence to a "tilt" toward Iraq in U.S. policy. On May 31, President Reagan in an interview in London noted that Iraq had confined its attacks against shipping in the Gulf whereas Iran had attacked ships belonging to neutral nations, and stated that "in time of war, the enemy's commerce and trade is a fair target if you can hurt them economically. So, in that sense, Iraq has not gone beyond bounds, as Iran has done."

Significantly, there currently exists a growing antipathy between Washington and Tehran as a result of Iranian-inspired Shi'ite terrorist efforts against U.S. personnel and installations in the Middle East. President Reagan on July 8, 1985, denounced Iran as a terrorist country.

A National Security Council study of October 1983 reportedly had concluded that U.S. interests would not be served if Iraq were to collapse. At the same time, it maintained that there was little the United States could do to aid Iraq directly. Iraq's primary needs, in order to sustain its ability to continue the war, were economic assistance and improvement in the morale of its officer corps. As a result of the study, the Administration reportedly has encouraged Gulf Arab states to increase financial support for Iraq and has conducted efforts aimed at limiting the flow of arms from third countries to Iran.

Iraq was removed from the list of countries supporting international terrorism in 1982, thereby facilitating sales of certain items of equipment formerly under restriction. In December 1982, a sale of some 60 civilian Hughes helicopters to Baghdad was reported. Iraq has been granted credit guarantees to finance sales of U.S. farm products since December 1982.

The U.S. and Iran

Since the hostage crisis, Washington has placed restrictions on trade between the United States and Iran, with the exception of food products and medical equipment. Nevertheless, newsmedia reports indicate that trade had increased, mainly on the basis of American firms trading through their overseas affiliates with Iranian organizations. But, on Jan. 23, 1984, the State Department added Iran to the list of countries reportedly supporting acts of international terrorism. A substantial illegal traffic in U.S. arms reportedly has developed in which American weapons and spare parts have been forwarded to Iran by a variety of routes. Iraqi officials in 1983 have claimed that Iran consistently has been receiving large quantities of U.S. weaponry through non-official sources and third countries, including South Korea and Israel, without interference from Washington. Iraqi Deputy Prime Minister Ramadan stated in February 1984 that he welcomed indications of "a more positive attitude" by the United States toward the matter. The State Department in March 1984 designated Ambassador-at-large Richard Fairbanks to coordinate U.S. efforts in limiting arms deliveries to Iran from Western Europe, Israel and friendly Asian states.

Such efforts reportedly have been successful in reducing the flow of spare parts and equipment. Within the United States, shipments of replacement parts for U.S. equipment destined for Iran from American firms have been seized. Since 1984, more than 70 persons have been arrested by U.S. authorities.

Following the Iranian attack on the Al-Faw Peninsula, a State Department spokesman warned Iran that an expansion of the conflict elsewhere in the Gulf regions would be a major threat to U.S. interests, noting that Iran had openly been conducting a campaign to intimidate moderate Gulf Arab states.

THE U.S. PROMOTES PEACE

Richard W. Murphy

Richard W. Murphy made the following comments in his capacity as Assistant Secretary, Bureau of Near Eastern and South Asian Affairs in the Department of Defense.

Points to Consider

1. How are U.S. interests in the Middle East defined?
2. How does the Iran-Iraq War threaten those interests?
3. Under what circumstances would the U.S. militarily intervene in the Gulf War?
4. How has U.S. policy tried to promote peace and avoid military intervention?

Excerpted from testimony by Richard W. Murphy before the House Committee on Foreign Affairs, June 11, 1984.

Our first priority in the conflict has been to achieve a ceasefire and the negotiation of a settlement through diplomatic means.

Our Middle East policy has long been based on our recognition that the region is a strategic crossroads between East and West and a source of energy for much of the free world, that Soviet dominance there would gravely disturb the worldwide strategic balance, and that we have close and historic ties with Israel and moderate Arab states in the area. Because of these basic interests, we have worked for over three decades to resolve regional conflicts and to seek a real peace between Israel and its Arab neighbors.

The war between Iran and Iraq, now in its fourth year, directly affects those interests. The continuing escalation in the Gulf threatens to widen the conflict, to curtail the Gulf's supply of oil to the West, and to endanger the security of our moderate Arab friends and the stability of the entire Middle East.

U.S. Policy

With that recognition, our policy consists of four crucial elements:

— The first is to ensure the free flow of oil to the West;

— Second, to contain the expansion of Soviet and other radical influence;

— Third, to maintain the security of the Arab states of the Gulf. These states, especially Saudi Arabia, are the physical and political barrier to Soviet and Iranian radical expansionism, as well as a force for moderation throughout the region.

— Finally, and equally important, whatever steps we take must complement our efforts to achieve peace between the Arab states and Israel. Our Middle Eastern policy is built on the premise that we can foster and encourage a secure, strong and confident Israel while, at the same time, helping to ensure that our moderate Arab friends have the support they need to maintain their own security. These two goals are not contradictory; they are complementary.

The Gulf War

Our objective is to bring the Gulf war to a negotiated end, in which neither belligerent is dominant, and in which the sovereignty and territorial integrity of both are preserved. It is our basic position that a victory by either side is neither militarily achievable nor strategically desirable because of its destabilizing effect on the region. Further, it is our objective to avoid direct U.S. military involvement in the war. We believe that a crucial factor in achieving that objective is to enable the Gulf states to defend themselves, rather than having to call for U.S. intervention for their protection.

Our first priority in the conflict, and that of our Allies and the Gulf states, has been to achieve a ceasefire and the negotiation of a settlement through diplomatic means. We have repeatedly urged restraint on both parties, directly with Iraq, and with Iran, through others who have access. We supported the efforts of the United Nations, including Resolution 552, which reaffirms the right of free navigation and calls on all parties to respect that right.

Military Intervention

We have no desire to intervene militarily in the Gulf. We have made that clear to our friends and to the Soviet Union. But we have also considered it prudent to consult closely with our allies on how we could cooperatively respond to contingencies, both in the political/military and energy spheres. We have discussed with the Gulf states, over many

A Negotiated Settlement

Our objective with respect to the Iraq-Iran war is to bring it to a negotiated end in which neither belligerent is dominant and in which the sovereignty and territorial integrity of both are preserved.

U.S. Department of State, June, 1984.

months, the threat they face, our common interest in meeting that threat, and how this could be done. We have made it known that we would not intervene unless asked to do so, and that we are not seeking such an invitation.

The current attacks on non-belligerent shipping to neutral ports directly threaten the Gulf states and also our own interests. Saudi Arabia has now been involved in aerial combat with Iran. If war were to be ignited among the states of the Gulf, the vulnerable oil and port facilities of those states would be endangered, along with a major share of the world's oil supply.

Some 20 to 25 percent of the oil consumed in the free world is produced in the Gulf, which is now exporting nearly 8 million barrels of oil per day, much of it to our allies in Europe and Asia. Although only three percent of our oil comes directly from the Gulf, we still import about one-third of our oil supply. Therefore, we are not isolated from the world oil market. Disruptions in the oil supply and a worldwide increase in prices could cut short the recovery now underway in our own economy and that of the rest of the world.

It was in view of this threat that we responded on an urgent basis to Saudi Arabia's request for Stinger air defense missiles, additional aerial refueling capability and accelerated delivery of fuel tanks to extend the flying time of the Saudi F-15's. Any lesser response would have seemed tentative, would possibly have emboldened, rather than deterred, Iran, and would have raised doubts about our determination and commitment to Gulf security. The President concluded that important national security interests justified his use of the special waiver authority. This decision was not taken lightly. The need was immediate and real, and the President acted accordingly. His decision clearly aids deterrence, not escalation.

The danger of the conflict spreading to the Gulf states was underscored by the shooting down by Saudi F-15's of at least one Iranian F-4. Because of the presence of U.S. AWACS and aerial tankers in Saudi Arabia, the incident raises important War Powers questions.

Conclusion

We have considered the information available to us, and based on that information, we have determined that no War Powers report is called for at this time. U.S. military aircraft and personnel in Saudi Arabia are not equipped for combat, have not been introduced into a situation of imminent hostilities, and have not been put in any danger of hostile action.

Our policy in the Gulf, during more than ten years and four administrations, has been to strengthen our friends' abilities to defend themselves while avoiding direct U.S. military involvement. We have been successful. Our security assistance program with Saudi Arabia, our cooperation with other states in the region, our military presence in the Arabian Sea, have all enhanced the confidence and capabilities of our friends. The tragic war in the Gulf has raged for almost five years. Not only has the oil continued to flow from the Gulf, but also our friends have been able to defend themselves without the presence of U.S. combat forces. These facts prove the validity of the objectives we established ten years ago and are witness to our effectiveness at meeting them.

U.S. POLICY PROMOTES WAR

Robert C. Johansen and Michael G. Renner

Robert C. Johansen is a senior fellow of the World Policy Institute and editor-in-chief of the quarterly WORLD POLICY JOURNAL. Michael G. Renner is research assistant to the senior fellow.

Points to Consider

1. How costly has the war been?
2. Why has the U.S. given economic assistance to Iraq?
3. What has U.S. policy been like toward Iran?
4. How is Soviet policy toward Iran and Iraq described?
5. What new U.S. policies could help end the war?

Robert C. Johansen and Michael G. Renner, "War without End in the Persian Gulf," *Christianity and Crisis,* December 9, 1985, pp. 496-499.

The Iran-Iraq war is now entering its sixth year. The conflict has killed nearly one million people, forced more than three million persons from their homes, caused several hundred billion dollars in property damage, imposed immense sacrifices, and devastated the perspectives for economic development in the two countries. The war jeopardizes international shipping in the Persian Gulf and international air travel over Iran, undermines time-honored norms against the use of poison gas and the inhumane treatment of prisoners of war, and periodically threatens to bring other countries, including the United States, more directly into the fighting.

Despite these staggering costs and serious dangers, the war continues because for one reason or another, Washington, Moscow, Tel Aviv, Damascus, and Riyadh believe that keeping the Iranians and Iraqis bogged down in the war will make them more docile and manageable. The belligerents' neighbors are content to have these two aspirants for regional hegemony exhaust each other rather than expand their influence into the Persian Gulf states. (These states, members of the Gulf Cooperation Council, are Saudi Arabia, Kuwait, Qatar, Bahrain, United Arab Emirates, and Oman.) Their primary security concerns rest with Iran's efforts to stir Shi'ite unrest in their own countries. To fend off this perceived threat and to preoccupy Baghdad they have encouraged Iraqi belligerence.

Oil supplies, particularly to its allies, are of immediate concern to the United States. Perceiving a Soviet invasion of Iran and the gulf as the main threat to supply security, Washington has sought to safeguard access to gulf oil by expanding its military presence in, and ties to, the states in the area, especially Saudi Arabia and Oman. U.S. officials also seek to regain influence with Iran, considered to be the prime "strategic prize" in the region by both superpowers because of its location, its natural resources, and its large domestic market. *U.S. policy makers hope that prolongation of the war will weaken Tehran and Baghdad and make them more susceptible to outside influence.* As Henry Kissinger explained, "the ultimate American interest in the war [is] that both should lose." The U.S. proclamation of "neutrality" in the face of Iraqi aggression is not only inappropriate, it is also an untrue characterization of U.S. policies. By tilting toward Iraq—tacitly supporting Iraq's invasion, sharing

116

military intelligence, and offering economic assistance—
Washington has not only sought to restrain Iran but also to
gain influence over the Iraqi leadership.

Although Moscow is intent on preserving its relationship
with Baghdad in the face of Western efforts to loosen Soviet-
Iraqi ties, it also has attemped—in vain—to improve its relationship with Tehran. As the invasion of Afghanistan
demonstrates, Moscow wants to prevent a string of radical
Islamic governments which owe their allegiance to Iran from
emerging along the Soviet periphery.

While professing this questionable "neutrality" in the Iran-
Iraq war, both superpowers have engaged in intricate
maneuvers to achieve several objectives: to court (or at least
not to alienate) the two combatants, to prevent either of
them from scoring a decisive victory, and to avoid being
eclipsed in the regional power game. Satellite monitoring
capabilities provide both Washington and Moscow with continuous information on troop strengths and battle plans for
Iran and Iraq. The influence derived from control of this information could be used to initiate and support a mediation
process. Instead, the superpowers have utilized the flow of

military goods and credits to both belligerents to fine-tune their war machines and prolong the fighting.

Why do Iran and Iraq continue to fight a war that not only fails to achieve any of its stated objectives, but shatters their societies and devastates their economies? The border dispute over the Shatt al-Arab estuary that helped ignite the war rapidly receded into the background, but the rivalry for hegemony in the region and the historical strains that run between the two societies continue to fuel the conflict....

That is not to say the war is popular. On the contrary, a weariness is growing among the two populations, and there are signs of dissension within the ruling circles of both countries. Iran has witnessed numerous demonstrations against the war, Iraq the execution of dissenting officials, while repression increases in both countries. The two governments can still count on the support, or at least the acquiescence of the majority of their populations. But faltering economies increase the apathy and discontent with the war.

A New Policy

It is time for a rethinking of policy. Recent Middle East history suggests that military policies in general, and this war in particular, are unlikely to secure for either superpower the influence they seek. Washington has been the leader in supplying arms to Middle East countries. Between 1950 and 1982 it sold $75 billion worth of weapons to the region. These weapons failed to keep the Shah in power. And the highly vulnerable oil wells, refineries, and loading stations cannot be protected militarily despite vast arsenals. As the war between Iran and Iraq continues, both countries will grow weaker, but both will rigorously resist becoming pawns of the superpowers.

The U.S. and the Soviet Union are less interested in the war itself than in the political trajectory of the regimes in Baghdad and Tehran. The fact that they are not aligned on opposite sides of the conflict demonstrates that Washington and Moscow do not have to fear being locked into a "zero-sum" game. The Soviet leadership has continually expressed interest in a multilateral effort to solve the conflicts in the Middle East, even while supplying large quantities of arms to Iraq.

Although it is allied with Baghdad, the Soviet Union has been critical of both belligerents: of Iraq because it started the war (Moscow even cut off military supplies during the first two years of the conflict), and of Iran because it carried the war into Iraq. Moreover, as long as the war continues, Moscow finds itself in a dilemma: It is trying to strengthen ties with two client states, Iraq and Syria, while Syria is allied with Iran.

Each belligerent has been receptive to peace initiatives when it perceived its own position as weak. Since its troops have been evicted from Iranian territory, Iraq has on several occasions said it was ready to accept a cease-fire. Conversely, during the first 20 months of the war, Iran's only condition for peace was a return to the prewar status quo. Invariably, however, the opponent has rejected any bid for peace because it felt confident enough it could gain an advantage.

It is just possible that U.S. diplomacy could gain Soviet support for a broad peace initiative if it avoids both the appearance and the reality of trying to reinforce U.S. military power in the gulf area. The timing of such an initiative is crucial. It can hope to meet with success only if it seizes the opportunity when both belligerents perceive their chances to win the war as limited or nonexistent. Since Iranian ground troops failed badly in their last offensive (May 1985), Tehran may be more accommodating toward efforts to negotiate an end to the war. In June, Ayatollah Khomeini reportedly ordered the Iranian forces to use "defensive" tactics. Iraq, on the other hand, is now incapable of carrying the tide of war far into Iranian territory....

To begin, the United States should undertake a major multilateral effort to restrain arms exports and other military and financial aid to both belligerents. If the United States approached the Soviet Union as an equal, Moscow might assist the effort to curtail arms exports. The United States should also press other suppliers to stop military shipments to Baghdad and Tehran. U.S. success in stopping its allies from supplying Iran with arms and spare parts demonstrates that, given sufficient political will, Washington can help slow the arms flow into the region.

The United States, Saudi Arabia, and its allies in the Gulf Cooperation Council cannot change Iran's behavior, over which they have little influence, if they do almost nothing to change Iraq's behavior, over which they can exert enormous leverage. The conservative gulf governments could curtail Baghdad's warfare by making their financial support ($1 billion per month) conditional on a halt in Iraq's assaults on tankers and Iranian air traffic, use of poison gas, and bombing of Iranian cities and towns. These restraints would meet Iranian conditions for a ceasefire along the prewar borders.

Second, the United States itself should substantially reduce its military commitments and presence in the gulf region. The U.S. government should also encourage its allies and invite the Soviet Union and its allies to scale down their military presence. U.S. and allied security can be well served by establishing a region free of all outside forces. An uninhibited flow of oil, purportedly the major concern of the Western powers, can be more effectively maintained through an evenhanded diplomacy and a stabilization of commercial relations than by U.S. military intervention.

To promote regional stability and reduce the danger of escalation in local conflicts, the superpowers should establish a mutual nonintervention agreement. Far from being a zero-sum game, one superpower's restraint holds the benefit of noninterference by the other. Either the United States or the Soviet Union could, without any negotiations, initiate the first phase of nonintervention by pledging to abide by the following principles in return for a similar promise from the other:

- to refrain from expanding existing military bases or from establishing new ones in the region;
- to deploy or transport no weapons of mass destruction within the region;
- to send no troops, even if invited, to countries in the region;
- to support international peacekeeping under a multilateral mandate, if external forces are required;
- to seek, with states in the region, to maintain genuine nonalignment and noninterference;
- to support open commerce and trade.

It is reasonable to expect that the Soviet Union would favor such an arrangement, since the late Soviet President Brezhnev included elements of a nonintervention agreement in a speech made in December 1980. Initially, the nonintervention accord should be focused on Iran and Iraq, and be spread as soon as feasible to include other countries in the region.

No Money, No War

Third, the United States should explore with major oil importers the possibility of complementing the multilateral effort to halt arms shipments by curtailing oil purchases from Iran and Iraq so long as they remain at war. The large oil revenues of the Middle East countries have fueled the arms race, as has the willingness of supplier states to sell them almost any weapon. In 1983, for example, Iran spent more than 70 percent of its oil revenues for military purposes; Iraq, in 1982, spent close to 80 percent. In fact, Iraq has received many weapons from France in direct exchange for oil.

Sharply reduced oil revenues would limit both regimes' ability to shop for weapons from noncomplying government suppliers and private arms dealers. Both might thus be more inclined to entertain serious peace overtures. Curtailing oil purchases would also dampen the threat of military escalation by reducing the advantage either side could possibly expect to gain through assaults on the opponent's oil exports and tankers. Since Iraq will soon be stepping up its oil exports through a new pipeline, such a measure would carry even greater weight. The purpose of such a boycott is simply to promote an end to the fighting. Consuming countries could promise to resume buying oil from Iran and Iraq, once peace is restored, in quantities at least as large as before the curtailment of purchases and at a fair price.

Fourth, the Western countries and the Soviet Union should stop deliveries on credit to Iraq and Iran of equipment useful to the war effort for as long as the war continues. Such a policy should be combined with a pledge to assist in the postwar reconstruction of both societies. Because outside credits are crucial in supporting the continuation of the war, such a policy would be an additional incentive to end it. The fundamental principle underlying all these initiatives is that the benefits of peace demonstrably outweigh the benefits of war....

In the meantime, the war goes on, people die, and the entire region is threatened. Because it is unrealistic to expect full international cooperation and implementation of the measures suggested here, it is important for the U.S. not to conclude that nothing can be done. On the contrary, if a few of the major suppliers of arms and money and the largest purchasers of oil begin to implement these policies, it could tip the balance away from further militarization and deterioration in the region and toward peace and stability. Then it may be possible to begin to demonstrate to all concerned that the benefits of peace do indeed outweigh the benefits of war.

19 THE WAR AND U.S. POLICY

U.S. POLICY OPTIONS:
IDEAS IN CONFLICT

The following article contains four possible options for U.S. policy toward the Iran-Iraq War.

Points to Consider

1. How might our national interest be served by a policy of non-intervention?
2. Why might U.S. military intervention in the Gulf War be a mistake?
3. How could U.S. interests be served by supporting Iraq?
4. Why might U.S. support for Iran be in America's long term interest?
5. What is meant by the term U.S. interests?

Wounded Child Beside Mother

MILITARY INTERVENTION MAY BE NEEDED

Stansfield Turner

The French are reported to be delivering jets armed with Exocet missiles to Iraq. The Iraqis are threatening to use them against Iran. The Iranians are threatening to interrupt the flow of Persian Gulf oil in response.

These threats have to be taken seriously. One quarter of the Free World's oil comes through the Persian Gulf. Despite the current oil surplus, the shock of an extended cutoff could make prices soar.

But there is reason to be skeptical, too. Iraq's Saddam Hussein may well be bluffing. And since he must worry about antagonizing his Saudi Arabian and other Persian Gulf supporters, he may think twice about the consequences of following through on his threats.

Whether Iran's Ayatollah Khomeini is bluffing is hard to predict; he's irrational. The bigger question is whether he could actually carry out his threat. It would be much easier for Iraq to hit a tanker with an Exocet missile than for Iran to block the Strait of Hormuz, which is 35 miles wide.

But if the threats become real, this country must act. We are the leader of the Free World. We must be concerned for the stability of Japan and our European allies, who depend on Persian Gulf oil.

And remember, Venezuelan and Nigerian oil reserves will run out. So will North Sea oil. The world's great oil reserves are largely in the Mideast. If the Soviets ever controlled them, they would gain substantial leverage.

If it becomes necessary, we and our allies must deploy naval power—several aircraft carriers, destroyers and minesweepers—to reassure any ships passing through the Gulf that they would not be vulnerable to attack.

Khomeini could cause insurance rates of oil tankers to soar just by making threats. A mere report that he had mined the Strait could cause panic. And one good missile in an oil-laden tanker could spoil your whole afternoon.

This country has very little influence with Iran. But in recent months, Iran has tried to reestablish economic relations with the West, so diplomatic pressure from our allies may be possible.

MILITARY INTERVENTION SHOULD BE AVOIDED

Sheldon L. Richman

President Reagan favors Iraq in its war with Iran and has vowed to use military force to keep the Strait of Hormuz safe from Iranian interference, but a far wiser policy can be stated in two words:

Stay out!

The American people have no reason to take sides in this 42-month-long war between two brutal despotisms. In fact, we have more important things to worry about.

No real interest would be achieved by our entry, but much would be risked.

Unfortunately, wars of conquest have been the rule in that region for centuries. Some battles have been religious, some political. The latest war is a mixture.

Iran is a fundamentalist Shiite Moslem theocracy; Iraq is a secular socialist state, in which a Sunni Moslem minority rules the Shiite majority. They are fighting over territory and religon.

U.S. intervention in this dispute, which is of little concern to us, would place the American people in the middle of a fanatical and bloody fight. The only predictable results would be intense resentment at such outside interference, a long involvement and many casualties. There is no way a rapid deployment force could pull off a quick, clean, surgical strike to clear the strait.

What about the oil?

First, Iran is not likely to close the strait, even if it could. It, too, sends oil through that passage. But if it did, U.S. intervention would not help.

If Iran's threats force up oil tanker insurance premiums, thereby stopping the flow of oil, it is hard to see how American forces could restore it. The intensified fighting would only continue to keep the tankers away.

This need not mean a new oil crisis for the West. The United States got only 3 percent of its oil from the Persian Gulf last year. We simply are not dependent on those imports. And one can't even predict higher oil prices with assurance if the strait is closed.

Most of our oil imports now come from Mexico, Canada, Venezuela, Great Britain and Indonesia. It stands to reason that a cutoff from the Persian Gulf would be made up in part by these producers. They would also supply Western Europe and Japan, which are dependent on the strait.

But even in the worst case, surely higher oil prices for us and the rest of the world's consumers are preferable to seeing Americans die in a full-scale war in an area largely irrelevant to us on the other side of the globe.

CONSIDERING U.S. SUPPORT FOR IRAN

Reuben A. Baumgart

The Iran–Iraq war is one of the great tragedies of modern history. Total war casualties for both sides may now be in excess of one million people. The war threatens the security and well-being of all Middle Eastern peoples as well as the two major superpowers, the United States and the Soviet Union. It also concerns the peace and security of the entire world since both the Soviet and the American leaders have military plans to intervene in the gulf war if either power feels that vital security interests demand military action.

The U.S. and the Soviet Union

The Soviet Union foresees potential trouble from the Iranian Islamic Republic. The Soviet Union has a large Moslem population bordering Iran and would not tolerate the export

Reuben A. Baumgart has been a feature writer for *The Milwaukee Journal, The Minneapolis Star and Tribune* and the *St. Paul Pioneer Press.*

of anti-Soviet Khomeini Islamic fundamentalism from Iran. The United States feels the Iranian Revolution's radical fundamentalism threatens the Middle Eastern pro-American monarchies like Saudi Arabia.

Both the United States and the Soviet Union have given lip service to the notion of neutrality in the gulf war, but in reality have favored the Iraqis with sales of military equipment. Both the United States and the Soviet Union want access to the oil of the Persian Gulf region and do not envision hostile Middle Eastern nations denying access to important oil reserves. It should also be noted that the oil reserves of the gulf region are more important to the United States than to the Soviets, since the Soviets are self-sufficient in oil, while the U.S. must import large quantities to meet its daily consumption needs.

Tilt Toward Iraq

In its policy toward the war, the United States has declared a concern for peace and called on the warring parties to negotiate a settlement to the conflict. The actual tilt toward Iraq, however, behind the words and rhetoric, may not serve long term interests of the American people for several reasons.

Iran is a dominant and important nation in the gulf region because of its size, population and rich oil reserves. Those reasons alone make it wise not to pursue a policy of hostile relationships for the long term. It is true that the hostage crisis was a bitter experience for Iranian-American relations, but so was World War II for all parties involved, and we now count our former enemies among our best friends and trading partners.

The Long View

With Iran and the entire Middle East, the long view is important. It is possible that Ayatolla Khomeini's Islamic fundamentalism may spread to all the countries of the Middle East with the exception of Israel. The pronounced anti-American character of the Iranian Revolution, and Islamic fundamentalism, are not reassuring for U.S. and Western influence in general. Iran, under the leadership of the Ayatollah Khomeini, is the first Middle Eastern nation to successfully oppose and throw out almost all Western influence and power.

Tilt Toward Iran

Given these future long term possibilities, it might be wise to consider opening the door to a less hostile relationship with Iran, and perhaps even a tilt favoring Iran, rather than Iraq in this bloody gulf war. Arms aid or sales would not necessarily have to be a part of this tilt, but rather it could take the form of policy statements, and improvements in trade arrangements and diplomatic exchanges at the embassy level. Should the Iranian Revolutionary ideas spread to other nations of the Persian Gulf, it would make sense for the United States to be on speaking terms with these strategically placed and oil-rich nations. It would certainly not seem in the American vital interest to be on the wrong side of dominant political forces in many Middle Eastern nations.

It is true that massive human rights violations have occurred in revolutionary Iran. But Americans must remember that Iraq has no better record on human rights than Iran, and that U.S. transnational corporations have over 15 billion dollars worth of assets in South Africa, considered by many to be the most evil government on the planet earth. A tilt toward Iran would not mean approval of their policies or human rights record. It would just mean a recognition by U.S. policy makers that Americans understand that they cannot control or oppose powerful political movements in the gulf region, and that the United States is willing to carry on normal diplomatic and trade relations with Iran and other countries when governments we do not approve of hold political power.

This policy might be the basis for a more sensible relationship between Iran and the United States. It could also give us some leverage with Iranian leaders should we wish to make attempts to moderate the anti-American and anti-Israeli policies of Islamic fundamentalism.

NATIONAL INTEREST LIES IN BACKING IRAQ

Christine Helms

The United States has myopically maintained neutrality in the Iran-Iraq war. Our self-interest requires a tilt toward Iraq.

Before Iran took Americans hostage, Washington believed, naively, that an early normalization of relations with Ayatollah Ruhollah Khomeini's regime was possible. Khomeini has followed his own course: neither alliance with the Soviet Union nor normalization with the United States.

Second, we have relied on the Arab states of the Persian Gulf to finance Iraq. But given both the duration of the war, which started in September 1980, and its high human cost—50,000 Iraqis dead, 60,000 wounded, 50,000 prisoners of war in a population only one-third the size of Iran's—those states' funding will not be sufficient to sustain Iraq indefinitely.

Third, the United States, believing that Iraq would not collapse, has assumed that a military stalemate that drains both countries serves our interests. In fact, a permanent stalemate is not certain.

We need Iraq for leverage against Syria, as we have almost none. Syria continues to maintain forces on its eastern border with Iraq, thereby limiting the number of Syrian forces threatening Lebanon and Israel. If Iraq collapses and a Syrian-Iranian axis is formed, Syria will become the new regional superpower.

The nightmare of a Syrian-Iranian axis would be felt not only in Israel and Lebanon, but also in the area around the Persian Gulf, through which passes at least a third of Europe's oil and half of Japan's.

U.S. policy makers' erroneous, stereotyped image of Iraq as radical and pro-Soviet has delayed rapprochement between Baghdad and Washington. Since 1975, however, Iraq's relations with the Soviet Union have deteriorated. Almost all Soviet advisers have been expelled.

In recent years, Iraq has probed for an improvement in relations with the United States. Washington has made only one request of Baghdad—that it restrain Abu Nidal, a Palestinian terrorist. Baghdad announced that it has done so, and Abu Nidal is now in Damascus.

Iraq has also agreed, unlike Syria, to invite Amnesty International representatives to discuss human-rights violations and means to resolve them. Still more important, President Saddam Hussein has told Rep. Stephen Solarz, D-N.Y., that he accepts Israel's right to secure borders.

The ever-strengthening ties of the Gulf Cooperation Council, comprising the Arab Gulf states, has been one of the most promising developments for Gulf security in recent years. Among other activities, it has planned joint military exercises and intelligence exchanges. The council has warned the Soviet Union to keep out of the Gulf, and has accepted U.S. military-access arrangements with Oman and Bahrain.

Washington has ignored these changes in the strategic situation and in Iraq, but there have been recent signs that the administration is exploring the Iraqi option.

Possible steps to assist Iraq are intelligence-sharing, repair of Iraq's oil facilities and assistance to export the oil, denial of further arms sales to Iran (from any source, including Israel), and active resistance to Iranian threats and terrorist activities in the region.

RECOGNIZING AUTHOR'S POINT OF VIEW

This activity may be used as an individualized study guide for students in libraries and resource centers or as a discussion catalyst in small group and classroom discussions.

Guidelines

Many readers do not make clear distinctions between descriptive articles that relate factual information and articles that express a point of view. Articles that express editorial commentary and analysis are featured in this book. Examine the following statements. Then try to decide if any of these statements take a similar position to any of the authors in chapter four. Working as individuals or in small groups, try to match the point of view in each statement below with the most appropriate author in chapter four. Mark the **appropriate reading number** in front of each statement. Mark (0) for any statement that cannot be associated with the point of view of any author in chapter four.

____ **Statement one:** The U.S. must be willing to use military force to protect the flow of oil from the gulf states to western nations.

____ **Statement two:** It would not be in the interest of the U.S. to use military force in the Middle East.

____ **Statement three:** The United States should help the Iraqi military defeat Iran.

____ **Statement four:** The ultimate American interest in the Iran-Iraq War is for both sides to lose.

____ **Statement five:** The U.S. has been the leader in supplying weapons to the Middle East countries.

____ **Statement six:** The great powers should undertake a major effort to halt all arms shipments to Iran and Iraq.

____ **Statement seven:** All nations should stop the purchase of oil from Iran and Iraq as long as the war continues.

____ **Statement eight:** The goal of American policy toward the Iran-Iraq War has been to bring the conflict to an end.

____ **Statement nine:** The U.S. should remain neutral in the Iran-Iraq War.

____ **Statement ten:** Over one million people have been killed in the gulf war.

BIBLIOGRAPHY

BOOKS, GOVERNMENT PUBLICATIONS AND DOCUMENTS

Aziz, Tariq. **The Iran-Iraq Conflict: Questions and Discussions** (London: Translation and Foreign Languages Publishing House, 1981).

El Azhary, M.S. ed. **The Iran-Iraq War: An Historical, Economic, and Political Analysis** (London: Croom Helm, 1984).

Fadhil al-Samarra i, Nizar. **The Iran-Iraq Conflict; A Reading Between the Lines** (Baghdad: Dar al-Ma mun for Trans. & Pub., 1982).

Faridani, H. **The Imposed War** (Tehran: Ministry of Islamic Guidance, 1983).

Grummon, Stephen R. **The Iran-Iraq War: Islam Embattled** (New York: Praeger, 1982).

Heller, Mark A. **The Iran-Iraq War: Implications for Third Parties** (Cambridge, MA: Center for International Affairs, 1984).

Hunter, Robert E. **U.S. Policy and the Iran-Iraq War** (Washington, D.C.: Middle East Institute, 1984).

Hussein, Saddam. **Thus We Should Fight Persians** (Baghdad: Dar al-Ma mun for Translation & Pub., 1983).

Mannetti, Lisa. **Iran and Iraq: Nations at War** (New York: F. Watts, 1986).

Maull, Hanns W. **The Iran-Iraq War: A Permanent Situation in the Gulf Region?** (Bonn, Germany: Research Inst. Friedrich-Ebert Stiftung, 1982).

Novik, Nimrod. **The War in the Gulf: Strategic Implications and Israeli Security: A Preliminary Assessment** (Tel Aviv: University of Tel Aviv, 1980).

Tahir-Kheli, Shirin and Shaheen Ayubi, eds. **The Iran-Iraq War: New Weapons, Old Conflicts** (New York: Praeger, 1983).

Developments in the Persian Gulf, June 1984. Committee on Foreign Affairs, House of Representatives (Washington, DC: GPO, 1984).

Effects of the Iraqi Imposed War on Iraq's Economy (Tehran: War Information Headquarters, 1984).

The Iraqi-Iranian Conflict: Documentary Dossier (Baghdad: Ministry of Foreign Affairs, Iraq, 1981).

The Iraqi-Iranian Dispute: Facts v. Allegations (Baghdad: Ministry of Foreign Affairs of the Republic of Iraq, 1980).

The Smoldering Fires Along the Gulf: Impact Upon the International System (Bonn: Research Inst. Friedrich-Ebert Stiftung, 1982).

War in the Gulf: A Staff Report. Committee on Foreign Relations, US Senate (Washington, DC: GPO, 1984).

World Petroleum Outlook—1984. *Hearing: Committee on Energy and Natural Resources, US Senate (Washington, DC: GPO, 1984).*

MAGAZINES AND NEWSPAPERS

Alpern, D.M. "Punch—and Counterpunch." **Newsweek,** March 25, 1985:64.

Barnes, J. "Lashing Iraq's Fighting Spirit." **U.S. News & World Report,** February 24, 1986:42-3.

Behr, E. "Back to Trench Warfare?" **Newsweek,** July 2, 1984:37.

Borrell, J. "War and Hardship in a Stern Land." **Time,** Aug. 26, 1985:30-1.

Clifton, T. "'I am Fighting for Iran—and for Islam.'" **Newsweek,** March 10, 1986:51.

Coyne, M. "Iran under the Ayatollah." **National Geographic,** July 1985:108-35.

Crozier, B. "Assets in the Middle East." **National Review,** Aug. 24, 1984:22.

Dudney, R.S. "America Flexes Muscles Behind the Scenes." **U.S. News & World Report,** June 18, 1984:28.

Ellis, W.S. "The New Face of Baghdad." **National Geographic,** January, 1985:80-109.

Frank, A. "Shopping the Great Satan (Iranian Arms Smugglers)." **Forbes,** Jan. 27, 1986:32-3.

Graham, D. and others. "Iran Readies an Onslaught—Before the Money Runs Out." **Business Week,** March 24, 1986:53.

Hiro, D. "Fire in the Gulf." **Nation,** March 10, 1984:276.

Horton, B. "Iraq vs. Iran—Who What and Why of a Long War." **U.S. News & World Report,** April 15, 1985:32.

Ismael, T.Y. and J.S. Ismael. "Iraq's Interrupted Revolution." **Current History,** January 1985:29-31.

Kaplan, R.D. "Bloodbath in Iraq." **New Republic,** April 9, 1984:21-3.

Mitchell, J. "A Conflict Out of Control." **Macleans,** April 8, 1985:24.

Moody, J. "Guardian of the Straight (Oman)." **Time,** Dec. 2, 1985:58.

Mullin, D. "For Iraq, Things are Suddenly Looking Up." **U.S. News & World Report,** Dec. 24, 1984:31-2.

Nordland, R. "Trying the Logic of Force (Iraq goes on offensive). **Newsweek,** February 11, 1985:47.

Ramazani, R.K. "Iran: Burying the Hatchet." **Foreign Policy,** fall, 1985:52-74.

Sciolino, E. "The Big Brother (S. Hussein)." **New York Times Magazine,** February 3, 1985:16-21.

Serrill, M.S. "Shift in a Bloody Stalemate." **Time,** March 3, 1986:50.

Smith, W.E. "Carnage in the Marshes." **Time,** April 1, 1985:40-1.

_____. "Clouds of Desperation (use of mustard gas by Iraq). **Time,** March 19, 1984:28-30.

Stengel, R. "Arming a Quiet Bystander (Kuwait). **Time,** July 2, 1984:32.

Trillin, C. "Uncivil Liberties." **Nation,** March 16, 1985:296.

Trimble, J. "Confodent Iraqis: Iranians Will Not Pass." **U.S. News & World Report,** July 9, 1984:33-4.

Utting, G. "Arming Iran and Iraq." **World Press Review,** June 1984:49-50.

Watson, R. "The Unholy War in the Persian Gulf." **Newsweek,** March 12, 1984:40-2.

Whitacker, M. "Teheran's Blunder: A Decisive Defeat?" **Newsweek,** April 1, 1985:36-8.

Wolfe, J.H. "The Forgotten War." **USA Today,** July 1985:9.

"Attacks on Ships in the Gulf Debated in the Security Council." **UN Monthly Chronicle,** May, 1984:5-10.

"Bomblets Away (Chilean-Iraqi connection)." **Time,** August 27, 1984:34.

"Can Heaven Wait?" **National Review,** June 15, 1984:15.

"Chemical Weapons in Iran: Confirmation by Specialists, Condemnation by Security Council." **UN Monthly Chronicle,** March 1984:3-6.

"Death by Air." **Time,** April 9, 1984:38.

"Dire Strait." **Nation,** June 2, 1984:659-60.

"Dying in the Rain (Iraqi use of chemical weapons)." **National Review,** April 6, 1984:19-20.

"Gas Warfare's Ominus Comeback." **US News & World Report,** March 19, 1984:11.

"The Gulf: Playing for Keeps." **Newsweek,** March 3, 1986:49.

"Iran-Iraq War Curtails Mideast Airline Service." **Aviation Week Space Technology,** March 25, 1985:34.

"Iran-Iraq War: Now It's Hell." **US News & World Report,** April 1, 1985:12.

"Report on UN Mission: Prisoners of War in Iran and Iraq." **UN Monthly Chronicle,** no. 2, 3, 5 1985:41-3.

"Shipping Attacks in Gulf Region." **UN Monthly Chronicle,** no. 1, 1985:14.